Water Quality and Ecology of Great South Bay
(Fire Island National Seashore Science Synthesis Paper)

Technical Report NPS/NER/NRTR—2005/019

Kenneth R. Hinga

Graduate School of Oceanography
University of Rhode Island
Narragansett, RI 02882

September 2005

U.S. Department of the Interior
National Park Service
Northeast Region
Boston, Massachusetts

This report was accomplished under Cooperative Agreement 1443CA4520-99-007, modification 22, with assistance from the NPS. The statements, findings, conclusions, recommendations, and data in this report are solely those of the author(s), and do not necessarily reflect the views of the U.S. Department of the Interior, National Park Service.

Please cite this publication as:

Hinga, K.R. September 2005. Water quality and ecology of Great South Bay (Fire Island National Seashore Science Synthesis Paper). Technical Report NPS/NER/NRTR—2005/019. National Park Service. Boston, MA.

PREFACE

FIRE ISLAND NATIONAL SEASHORE
Science Synthesis Papers to Support Preparation of a
General Management Plan

BACKGROUND AND PURPOSE

Fire Island National Seashore (FIIS) is scheduled to begin preparation of a new General Management Plan (GMP) in the near future. A GMP outlines how natural and cultural resources, public uses, and park operations should be managed over the next several decades. The GMP addresses significant issues or challenges that are facing the park, proposes management solutions, and establishes management priorities. The Fire Island GMP will be prepared by a team of planners, with input from the park, technical subject matter experts, and with substantial public involvement.

To insure that the GMP team has all relevant natural resource information available to them, a series of scientific synthesis papers has been prepared for a variety of natural resource topics that will be of special relevance to the Fire Island GMP. Based on a 2-day meeting with the FIIS Superintendent, FIIS Chief of Natural Resource Management, Northeast Region planners, and Northeast Region science staff, the following natural resource topic areas were identified;

- Geomorphology of beaches and dunes
- Physical processes of the bay shoreline
- Habitat ecology and water quality of Great South Bay
- Conservation of Living Marine Resources (habitats, finfish and shellfish)
- Vector-borne diseases
- White-tailed Deer ecology and management

For each of these topics, leading scientific experts were invited to prepare papers that synthesize our current state-of-knowledge. There is a wealth of published technical information on these topics. The purpose of these papers was to provide a scientifically credible summary of the available and relevant information and present this information in a succinct manner. The GMP team will receive papers that provide an objective, independent and expert synthesis of an extensive and often complex technical literature. Each paper was subject to the scientific peer review process.

Each synthesis paper is expected to accomplish the following;

- Synthesize and interpret the relevant literature and monitoring data to describe the fundamental processes controlling the natural resource, and describe historic and recent trends or rates of change for relevant processes, habitats, or species.
- Describe current and historic management, regulatory, and other activities that have been relevant to the particular natural resource.
- Identify gaps in our current understanding of the natural resource.

Because the synthesis papers are prepared prior to initiation of the GMP process, if information gaps are considered critical to decision-making for the GMP there may be adequate time to conduct the appropriate required studies or data analysis tasks. Moreover, the papers will serve to identify topics or issues that should be the focus of additional synthesis or review papers in support of the GMP information gathering and synthesis phase.

OVERVIEW OF THE PAPERS

These summaries are derived, with some editing, directly from the individual papers.

The Coastal Geomorphology of Fire Island: a Portrait of Continuity and Change
Technical Report NPS/NER/NRTR—2005/021
Authors: Norbert P. Psuty, Michele Grace, and Jeffrey P. Pace
                Rutgers University
Summary: Fire Island has a well-developed beach on the ocean side and is dominated by a variety of dune features, reaching elevations of 11-13m. Much of the island is undeveloped and retains a wide array of coastal dune forms in near natural condition. However, there are a number of residential communities, primarily on the western portion of Fire Island, that have altered the landscape and geomorphological processes. The controlled inlets at either end of the island are a type of interactive feature that have particular roles in the passage of sand along the shore. Thus, the geomorphological characteristics and configuration of the island are products of a suite of natural processes, complemented by human actions. This paper describes the landforms (beaches, dunes, inlets, and barrier island gaps) and basic controls on these landforms, such as tides, wave climate, storm history, the availability and rate of supply of sediment, and sea level rise.

There is insufficient sediment coming to Fire Island from all of the potential sources to maintain the entire system. There is evidence of erosion on all parts of the island, except the artificially-created Democrat Point. The sediment deficits are greatest along the eastern portion of the island, but are buffered in the central and western area because of the contributions from an offshore source. The recent acceleration in sea-level rise, coupled with the general negative sediment budget, will result in continued beach erosion and dune displacement, with greater effects occurring in the eastern portion of the island.

During the peer review process, it was determined that a follow-up synthesis paper should be prepared that specifically focuses on the response of Fire Island beaches and dunes to human activities, including ORV traffic, structures, sand fencing, beach scraping, and other activities. This paper is presently being developed.

Bay Shoreline Physical Processes, Fire Island
Technical Report NPS/NER/NRTR—2005/020
Authors: Karl F. Nordstrom, Rutgers University
                Nancy L. Jackson, New Jersey Institute of Technology
Summary: Wave and current energies on the bay side of Fire Island are low, but much of the bay shoreline is eroding. The greatest changes occur near inlets or next to marinas and bulkheads. Inlets, overwash and dune migration deliver sediment from the ocean to the bay where it forms substrate that evolves into tidal flats, marshes and beaches. These sediment

inputs allow barrier islands to maintain themselves as they migrate landward under the influence of sea level rise. The creation and migration of inlets in the past extended their influence well beyond locations of present inlets.

About 17.0 km of the 49.5 km long bay shoreline of Fire Island is marsh; 24.5 km is beach; and 8.0 km is fronted by bulkheads, marina breakwaters and docks. The biggest constraints to allowing Fire Island to undergo natural dynamism are the desire to protect private properties on the island from erosion and overwash and the need to protect the mainland from flooding due to formation of new inlets. Bulkheads are common on the bay shore in developed communities. These structures replace natural formations landward of them and prevent sand from entering the littoral drift system, causing sediment starvation in unprotected areas downdrift. These adverse effects can be reduced by replacing lost sediment by beach nourishment. Use of beach fill on the low tide terrace covers benthic habitat. This problem could be avoided by placing fill above the mean high water mark, creating an eroding feeder upland.

Dune building projects on the oceanside and construction of bulkheads on the bayside restrict the delivery of sediment by inlets, wave overwash and aeolian transport. Temporary inlets would provide some sediment, but artificial closure by human efforts would limit these inputs to a much smaller area than in the past.

Future sea levels are expected to rise at a greater rate, causing increased frequency of overwash and creation of new inlets if not prevented by beach nourishment and dune-building projects on the oceanside. Elimination of the delivery of sediment to the bayside by these natural processes will result in continued retreat of the bay shoreline into the higher portions of the barrier island, resulting in loss of marsh habitat, increase in open water habitat, and truncation of cross-shore environmental gradients.

Water Quality and Ecology of Great South Bay
Technical Report NPS/NER/NRTR—2005/019
Author: Kenneth R. Hinga
             University of Rhode Island

Summary: The overall objective of this paper is to present a short synopsis of information on the characteristics of water quality and ecology of the Great South Bay, with particular attention to the waters within the boundaries of Fire Island National Seashore (FIIS), where possible. This report serves as an update and addition to the report *Estuarine Resources of the Fire Island National Seashore and Vicinity* (Bokuniewicz et al., 1993). Great South Bay is approximately 45 km long, with a maximum width of about 11 km. The Bay is shallow, with an average depth at mean low water of just 1.3m.

Regarding water quality, a review of bacterial indicator monitoring data suggests that some bayside beaches and marinas of Fire Island have had fecal coliform concentrations that are at or approaching levels of concern, but in general the levels are quite acceptable. Nutrient enrichment is an issue for all shallow, enclosed, lagoon-type estuaries, like Great South Bay. There is an encouraging trend of decreasing dissolved inorganic nitrogen in Great South Bay over the past quarter century. Coincident with the decline in nitrogen, there appears to be a trend of decreasing primary production, as determined by measuring phytoplankton chlorophyll concentration, over the past 15 years. Historically, portions of Great South Bay (e.g., near and in Moriches Bay) experienced intense phytoplankton blooms, probably attributed to discharges from duck farms. Since 1985, a brown tide has occurred periodically to disruptive levels in the Bay. Brown tide blooms can cause significant mortalities of hard clams and can damage seagrass beds because the blooms prevent light sufficient to support growth of the seagrass species. The densest seagrass beds in the Bay are found along the shallow shoreline of the Seashore.

Conservation and Management of Living Marine Resources
Technical Report NPS/NER/NRTR—2005/023
Authors: David O. Conover, Robert Cerrato, and William Wise
              Stony Brook University
Summary: The finfish species likely to be landed by commercial harvesters from Fire Island NS or nearby waters are bluefish, winter flounder, summer flounder, weakfish, Atlantic silversides, and menhaden. The recreational species landed within the Bay have not been described in detail since the 1960s, but total recreational landings for New York as a whole suggest that fluke, winter flounder, bluefish, weakfish, tautog, and black sea bass are the main species. Some of the fish species landed in the Seashore region are present only transiently as older juveniles and adults. Such species would include striped bass, menhaden, eels, and weakfish. These species do not use the Bay as a spawning and nursery area. Other species use Fire Island waters as both nursery grounds for young-of-the-year (YOY) stages as well as adults. The value of Seashore estuarine habitats for these species is great (bluefish, winter flounder, fluke, tautog, black sea bass). Ecologically important species, those that are an important forage species for piscivorous fishes, include Atlantic silversides, bay anchovy, sand lance, northern pipefish, and others. Killifishes are a major component of the fish fauna of salt marsh habitats. Shellfish of potential recreational or commercial value found within Seashore boundaries include surfclam, hard clam, blue mussel, soft clam, oyster, bay scallop, razor clam, conch, blue crab, Jonah crab, rock crab, lady crab, spider crab, and horseshoe crab (although not technically classified as shellfish). Generally, there has been a dramatic decline in the commercial harvest of shellfish species from the Bay. For example, since 1976 the harvest of hard clams has declined 100 fold. It is recommended that the Seashore take a leadership role in reaching out cooperatively to government and non-government agencies toward encouraging restoration of Great South Bay living marine resources and increasing public awareness of coastal zone management issues.

Vector-borne Diseases on Fire Island
Technical Report NPS/NER/NRTR—2005/018
Author: Howard S. Ginsberg
             USGS-Patuxent Wildlife Research Center
Summary: This paper discusses eleven tick-borne and five mosquito-borne pathogens that are known to occur at FIIS, or could potentially occur. The potential for future occurrence, and ecological factors that influence occurrence, are assessed for each disease. Lyme disease is the most common vector-borne disease on Fire Island. The Lyme spirochete, *Borrelia burgdorferi*, is endemic in local tick and wildlife populations. Public education, personal precautions against tick bite, and prompt treatment of early-stage infections can help manage the risk of Lyme disease on Fire Island. The pathogens that cause Human Monocytic Ehrlichiosis and Tularemia have been isolated from ticks or wildlife on Fire Island, and conditions suggest that other tick-borne diseases (including Babesiosis, Rocky Mountain

Spotted Fever, and Human Granulocytic Ehrlichiosis) might also occur, but these are far less common than Lyme disease, if present.

West Nile Virus (WNV) is the primary mosquito-borne human pathogen that is known to occur on Fire Island. Ecological conditions and recent epizootiological events suggest that WNV occurs in foci that can shift from year to year. Therefore, a surveillance program with appropriate responses to increasing epizootic activity can help manage the risk of WNV transmission on Fire Island.

<u>White-tailed Deer Ecology and Management on Fire Island</u>
Technical Report NPS/NER/NRTR—2005/022
Author: H. Brian Underwood
                 USGS-Patuxent Wildlife Research Center
Summary: Deer populations have grown dramatically on Fire Island National Seashore (FIIS) since 1983. Trend data reveal a dichotomy in deer dynamics. In the eastern half of the island, deer density appears to have stabilized between 25-35 deer/km^2. In the western half of the island, deer densities are 3-4 times as high in residential communities. Concomitant with that increase has been a general decline in physical stature of some animals, visible impacts on island vegetation, especially in the Sunken Forest, and a perceived increase in the frequency of human and deer interactions. Intensive research on FIIS has shown that deer occupy relatively predictable home ranges throughout the year, but can and do move up and down the island. Impacts of deer on vegetation are most dramatic in the Sunken Forest. Most obvious are the effects of browsing on the herb layer of the Sunken Forest. The least obvious, but perhaps more significant impact is the stark lack of regeneration of canopy tree species since about 1970, which coincides with the initiation of the deer population irruption. A number of herbs and shrubs have been greatly reduced in the understory, and their propagules from the soil.

Deer do not readily transmit the bacterium that causes Lyme disease to other organisms, but deer are important hosts for adult ticks which underscores their importance in the transmission pathway of the disease to humans. Deer on FIIS, while occasionally docile, are still wild animals and should be treated as such. Some animals are relatively unafraid of humans due to the absence of predation and a lack of harassment. This in turn has contributed to a long-standing tradition of feeding deer by many residents and visitors, particularly in western portions of the island. Feeding affects both the behavior and population dynamics of deer inhabiting Fire Island. Recent efforts to reduce deer feeding by visitors and residents have been very effective. Ongoing experiments with Porcine Zona Pellucida immunocontraception demonstrate some promise of this technology as a population management tool. Success appears to be linked directly to factors affecting access to deer, which vary considerably among treatment locations. Continued high National Park Service visibility among communities in the form of interpretive programs, extension and outreach activities, and continued support of research and monitoring of deer and their effects on island biota are keys to successful resolution of persistent issues.

Preface prepared by:
Charles T. Roman
National Park Service
North Atlantic Coast Cooperative Ecosystem Studies Unit

TABLE OF CONTENTS

PREFACE...iii

TABLE OF CONTENTS ix

INTRODUCTION 1

    General Characteristics Of Great South Bay 1

    A Changing Environment 3

WATER QUALITY 8

    Bacterial Contamination 8

    Chemical Contaminants 8

    Eutrophication: Nutrients and Oxygen..9

BIOLOGICAL RESOURCES 22

    Primary Production and Plant Abundance 22

    Brown Tides..22

BENTHIC HABITAT TYPES 26

    Submerged Aquatic Vegetation...26

    Unvegetated Benthos: Hard Clam Habitat..27

    Commercial and Recreational Harvests 28

    Hard Clams and Other Bivalve Mollusks 29

    Crustacea..29

    Finfish..30

RESEARCH NEEDS 34

ACKNOWLEDGEMENTS 35

LITERATURE CITED 36

INTRODUCTION

The overall objective of the report is to present a short synopsis of information on the characteristics of water quality and ecology of the Great South Bay, with particular attention to the waters within the boundaries of Fire Island National Seashore (FINS), where possible. This report serves as an update and addition to the report *Estuarine Resources of the Fire Island National Seashore and Vicinity* (Bokuniewicz et al., 1993). The intended audience is park planers and others involved in preparation of a FIIS General Management Plan who will need to consider the ecological characteristics of the waters of the park, but who are not necessarily marine ecologists or marine chemists.

This report does not attempt to duplicate or incorporate the prior review of Bokuniewicz et al. (1993), which is significantly longer than this report, even though the prior report does not extensively cover water quality issues. The interested reader who desires more detail than is provided in this report is advised to consult the Bokuniewicz et al. (1993) report. A reader looking for a thorough introduction to the characteristics of Great South Bay would do well to start by reading the fine review *The Great South Bay* by Schubel et al. (1991). Of more recent vintage, an introduction to the Long Island South Shore Estuary (the combination of South Oyster Bay, Great South Bay, Moriches Bay, and Shinnecock Bay) may be found in documents, especially the management plan pertaining to the State of New York initiative *The South Shore Estuary Reserve* at http://www.estuary.cog.ny.us./.

General Characteristics Of Great South Bay

Fire Island and Great South Bay (GSB) comprise a barrier island and lagoon system (Figure 1). Similar barrier island-lagoon systems mark the coastline of the eastern United States from Cape Cod to south of Cape Hatteras. On a geologic time scale, both Fire Island and Great South Bay are ephemeral features, constantly being reshaped by geologic processes and, in recent times, by human activities. Fire Island is built primarily from sands deposited during the last glacial period, when sea level was about 120 meters lower than present, and the shoreline of the Atlantic Ocean was some 150 kilometers to the south of what is now Long Island (Bokuniewicz and Schubel, 1991).

Roughly 7500 years ago, a predecessor to Fire Island was formed about 2 km south of the present shoreline. As sea level rose, the Island and the lagoon behind it migrated to its present position (Bokuniewicz and Schubel, 1991).

Fire Island is presently 48 km long (Fire Island Inlet to Moriches Inlet) and typically 300 to 500 meters wide. The dimensions of Great South Bay depend upon the boundaries one accepts for the Bay. GSB is contiguous with South Oyster Bay to the west and connects through a narrows to Moriches Bay to the east. When considering the circulation or ecology of GSB, establishing a firm boundary similar to a political boundary is not usually appropriate. With those qualifiers, GSB is approximately 45 km long (from Elder and Thatch Islands in the west to Smith Point in the east). At is maximum width south of the Bayshore community, GSB is 11 km wide. The surface area of the Bay is approximately 235 km^2 and the average mean low water depth is 1.3 m. (Wilson et al., 1991). It should be noted that many of the studies of GSB are driven by the limits set by political boundaries so it is rare to see studies of the Bay, or as the connected series of bays as a whole.

The floor of GSB is primarily sand, with a few sections in the northern side having a muddy bottom. There are also patches of sandy mud and areas marked by shell debris.

The waters of GSB are estuarine. That is, they are a region where salt and fresh waters mix. At present, the salinity of the GSB is most typically in the range of 25 to 30 parts-per-thousand. The offshore ocean waters are typically 31.5 parts-per-thousand. Fresh water from Long Island (and to a minor extent from Fire Island) delivered to GSB by streams and groundwater dilute the offshore salt water to the salinity found in GSB. The salinity is important to the ecology of the GSB, as the salinity is a major factor influencing which species can propagate or survive there. GSB has the highest salinity near the inlets, especially Fire Island Inlet. The salinity at a typical station varies somewhat (Table 1, Figure 2) depending upon the amount of recent precipitation. At a typical station, most salinity measurements fall within 2 parts-per-thousand of the median value. About 10 to 15% of the measurements may fall higher or lower than this normal range.

Temperatures in GSB vary seasonally (Figure 3). Summer surface-water temperatures typically reach 25 to 26 °C, with occasional measurements up to 29 °C. Winter temperatures have not been measured nearly as often, but temperatures at 0 to 2 °C appear common, with temperatures going below -1°C in exceptionally cold years. (The freezing point of 27 part-per-thousand salinity water is approximately -1.5 °C.)

Being a shallow system, there is often enough wind energy to mix the waters vertically. GSB is generally referred to as being unstratified. However, there is some evidence of stratification in that there are differences between surface and bottom temperatures and oxygen concentrations (differences greater than can be attributed to measurement uncertainty) for about 20-30% of the stations.

One important property of estuarine circulation is the concept of residence time. In general terms, residence time is the amount of time it takes for the water in an estuary to be replaced by new water coming into the estuary from offshore, from rivers, and from groundwater. Residence time indicates how fast the waters are flushed, and therefore a measure of how fast contaminants, nutrient fertilizers, and organisms themselves, may be removed from the estuary. Of course, not all parcels of water remain in an estuary for the same amount of time. Some parcels may come in with an incoming tide and immediately exit with the outgoing tide. Another parcel of water may come in with the tide and be mixed into the interior of the estuary and remain for many tidal cycles before exiting the estuary. Residence times are calculated using the amount of fresh water in the estuary as if it were a tracer or dye. The volume of freshwater in the estuary (determined from the salinity off the estuarine waters) divided by the rate of freshwater input (volume per day) provides the residence time. The rate of fresh water input varies with recent rainfall, and the responding variability in the salinity distribution of the estuary changes the amount of mixing, so the residence time varies somewhat in response to recent climatic conditions (see Pilson, 1985).

Taking the average salinity of GSB to be 25.9 parts-per-thousand (Tanski et al., 2001) and the salinity of ocean waters mixing into GSB to be 31.4 parts-per-thousand (Table 1), freshwater input to be 9.8×10^8 liters/day (Saville, 1962), an average residence time of about 50 days is found for GSB. Using somewhat different assumptions for the dimensions of GSB, Conley (2000) calculated a residence time of 96 days.

A Changing Environment

While the general migration of the island to the north over the last many thousand years is slow relative to a human life span, there are changes to the Island and Bay which are rapid enough to be observed during recent recorded history or a single lifetime. The west-most point of Fire Island, at the Fire Island Inlet (the passage between Fire Island and Jones Beach Island), migrated seven kilometers between 1825 and 1958 by the addition of sands being deposited at the west end of the island (see Kana, 1955). This is an average of 54 meters per year. The sands are transported westward along the ocean (south) side of the Island by longshore transport process that are a result of prevailing wave and current conditions.

Very short-term movements can also occur, usually induced by a major storm. These include beach erosion events, and perhaps more significantly, the opening of new inlets or breaches through the barrier island to the lagoon.

It is estimated that there have been 28 inlets through Fire Island over the last 300 years (Leatherman, 1985). When inlets open or close, the rates of exchange of water between the estuary and the offshore change. It follows that there are then changes in the residence time and salinity of water, which in turn may affect the organisms living in the estuary. Most of the historical inlets were at Westhampton Beach (part of the barrier Island at Moriches Bay. Recent studies indicate that the most probable places for breaches in Fire Island are at Old Inlet and Barret Beach (Conley, 2000). Modeling of the water flow expected if there was a breach at these locations indicates that a breach would raise the average salinity of GSB from 25.9 to about 29.5 parts-per-thousand. The residence time of the Bay would also be reduced by roughly half (from 96 to 40 or 52 days, depending upon the location of the inlet).

An example of the effects of a new inlet on the biology of GSB is provided by the opening of Moriches inlet in 1931. The barrier beach at Moriches Bay was breached by a storm creating Moriches inlet. The resultant increase in salinity in GSB permitted oyster predators to flourish that were previously excluded by low salinities. This is thought to have been a factor in the decline of the oyster harvests that were renown from GSB for the latter half of the 1800s and the early 1900s.

The biology of GSB has undergone some marked changes over time. Some of these changes may have been caused by anthropogenic factors (including harvesting of shellfish and finfish), but others remain to be explained satisfactorily. In a 1907 survey, the phytoplankton of GSB was dominated by diatoms. By the 1930s, extensive "small forms" or "green tides" of phytoplankton began to appear. The cause of these blooms was attributed to discharges from duck farms, especially in Moriches Bay. One way to deal with the problem was to keep open Moriches inlet (which had naturally closed between 1951 and 1953) to help flush out the organisms (Carpenter et al., 1991). Beginning in 1985, another type of nuisance bloom, the brown tide, appeared in GSB (and a number of other north east bays). It has been important, if not dominant, in the dynamics of GSB ever since (Cosper et al., 1987: Bricelj and Lonsdale, 1997). The brown tide organism, *Aureococcus anophagefferens*, is a poor food source for herbivores and appears to interfere with the ingestion of more suitable phytoplankton by herbivores. Brown tides have been recurring at nuisance levels in GSB, unlike some of the other estuaries in which it first appeared where blooms only reached nuisance levels in 1985. The etiology of brown tide blooms has yet to be resolved. Another example of biological change can be found in predators. GSB was once a traditional breeding ground for sandbar sharks, and pregnant females were caught frequently in the early 1900s. Now however, the GSB is not within the range of breeding grounds for the sandbar shark in the western North Atlantic (Merson 1998).

Even without major changes in GSB due to changes in circulation, one must expect the biology of the Bay to be subject to significant, and often unpredictable, changes over time. The most obvious example is the appearance, and recurrence, of the brown tides. Commercial and recreational fishing pressures significantly influence populations over time. The major harvests of oysters and hard clams could both be described as a pulse fishery (albeit decades long each) rather than as a very long term stable fishery. Hard clam commercial production dominated the industry before the turn of the century and went through major peaks of production in the 1940s and 1970s (with severe reductions in production in intervening periods).

Between 1954 and 1971, Long Island lost 47% of its wetlands, important habitat for many juvenile species (Green, 1972, Koppelman, 1991). It is also known that disease organisms can cause major shifts in populations. Most of the eelgrass in the Bay disappeared during the 1930s due to a wasting disease (as it did throughout much of the US East Coast; Short et al., 1987). The sewage management practices on Long Island have changed over time, and this appears to be having an effect on the nutrient loadings to the Bay. Regardless, if the cause is the influence of natural processes or human activities, one must expect that a decade or two into the future the biology of GSB will look, in some way, significantly different than it does today.

Figure 1 Station location map.

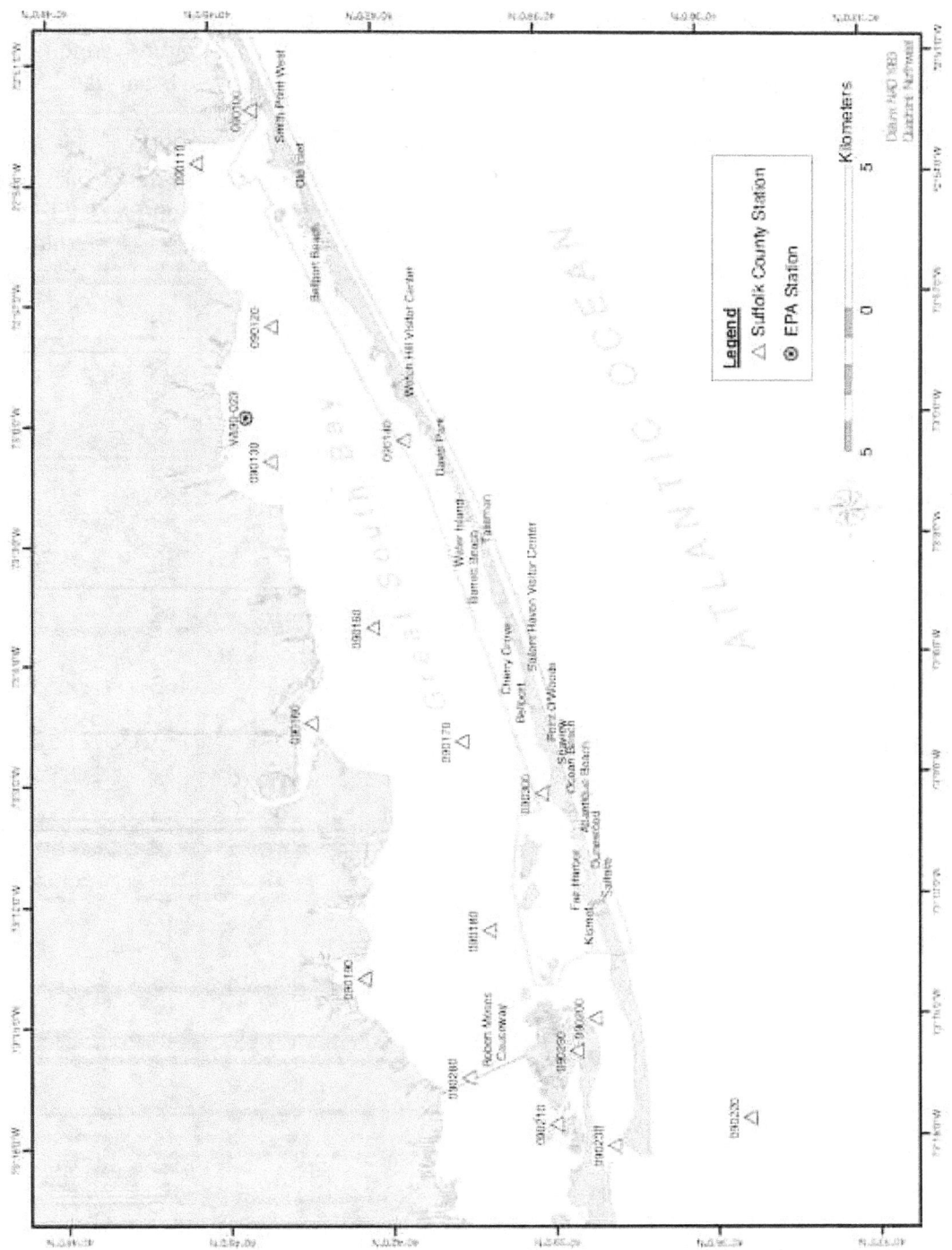

Table 1. Salinity and temperature summary from Suffolk County sampling program (Suffolk county, 2003). Sampling covers the period from September 1976 to December 2002 except for station 090300 that was begun in 1979. Sampling in most years was weekly or every other week through primarily the non-winter months. The low temperature range is not well documented as sampling was conducted only infrequently in January, February and March.

Station	090170 Central GSB north of Point O'woods	090100 Channel near Smith's Point	0900140 Off Davis Park	090300 Off Ocean Beach	090200 In Fire Island Inlet	090220 Offshore, 2.5 mi. south of Fire Island Inlet
Median Salinity	27.34	25.35	26.19	28.14	29.65	31.44
Maximum salinity	31.20	31.50	30.21	31.30	33.00	33.50
Minimum salinity	21.33	20.42	19.98	17.58	23.97	29.45
No. of salinity measurements	287	111	92	69	256	70
Maximum temperature	29.0	29.1	28.2	27.7	27.6	24.9
Minimum temperature	-0.8	-1.3	-1.2	-0.7	-0.3	1.6
Number of temperature measurements	420	132	120	103	368	91

Figure 2. Frequency of salinity measurements at station 090170 in central GSB. Data is from Suffolk County, 1993.

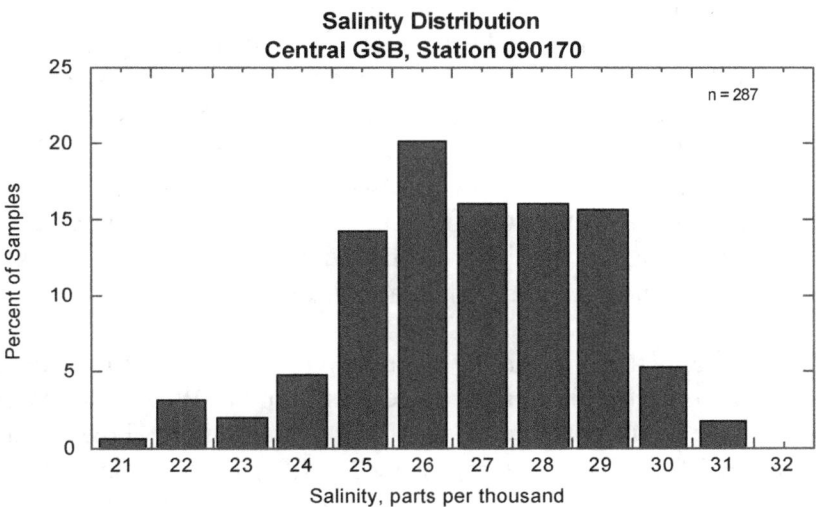

Figure 3. Surface water temperature over time at a station in central Great South Bay.

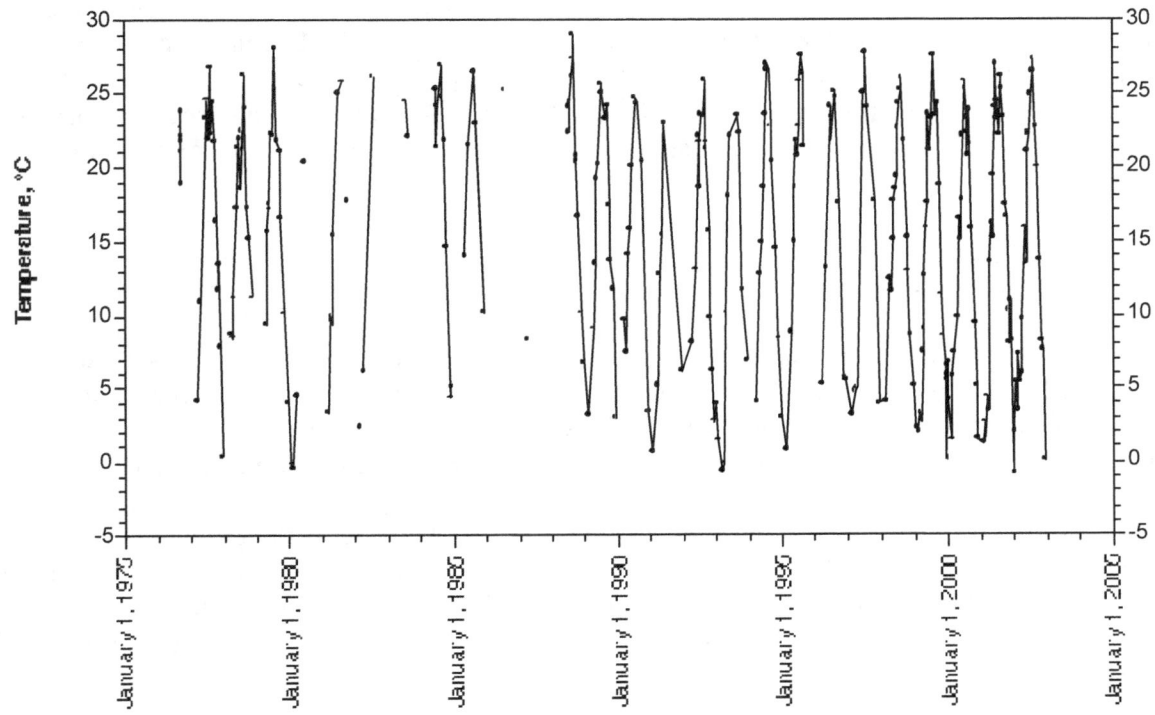

WATER QUALITY

Bacterial Contamination

Many of the beaches of Fire Island, both on the ocean and bay sides, have been monitored at least occasionally for indicator bacteria of fecal contamination. Table 2 is a summary of fecal coliform monitoring results for ocean-side beaches on Fire Island. Using fecal coliforms as a measure, the beaches on the ocean side have been found to be of excellent water quality, with only rare samples above a levels exceeding relevant standards. The New York State Sanitary Code stipulates that the bacteriological water quality of bathing beaches shall meet either a total coliform or fecal coliform standard. For fecal coliforms, the standard is fecal coliform MPN will not exceed 400 per 100 ml from five successive samples collected daily on five different days. (A more stringent standard is applied to shellfish harvesting areas. For shellfish harvesting, the NY standard is median fecal coliform MPN of 14 or less per 100 ml.)

On the bay side of the island there is clearly a greater presence of contamination by fecal coliforms (Table 3). The highest multi-year average was found at Watch Hill Marina (but that site does not appear to have been monitored since 1988). The Sailors Haven Marina also had elevated levels of fecal coliforms, and the report by NcNulty (1989) concluded that boating sources were the greatest sources of fecal contamination. Monitoring by Suffolk County in 1989 and 1990 (reported via Anon. 1992) indicates that some of the beaches on the bay side communities at the western extent of the National Seashore had fecal coliform concentrations that are at or approaching levels of concern. However, more recent monitoring by Suffolk

County gives much lower average values for fecal coliforms at some of the same beaches monitored in 1989 and 1990. It is not possible to state if this reduction is a true reduction or a change in methodology. Regardless, it is evident that fecal coliform levels on the bay side are still generally very good. One station of particular interest is at the Ocean Beach sewage treatment plant outfall. Coliform counts at this station do not appear to be any higher than at other locations along the north shore of Fire Island. Overall, it would seem advisable to initiate new monitoring of marinas and mooring areas, and to continue monitoring of the western community beaches.

Chemical Contaminants

Levels of chemical contaminants in the water and sediments appear to have been studied in GSB (at least in the vicinity of Fire Island) only rarely. The EPA EMAP program had one station in northern GSB in 1990 that provides measurements of a suite of chemicals in the sediments. (There were additional single stations in Moriches Bay and in Shinnecock Bay) A recent EPA National Coastal Assessment program has already taken new stations in GSB, but those results are not available at the time of the writing of this report. A study encompassing a number of stations in GSB measured dissolved trace metals in surface waters in 1998 and 1999 (Clark, 2000). Together, these studies provide a limited, but because of the general levels of contamination found, a useful picture of the levels of chemical contamination in GSB.

Clark (2000) measured the concentrations of four dissolved trace metals of interest at stations throughout GSB (Table 4). To put the measured levels in perspective, it is useful to compare the measured values to values of these metals which will likely result in some biological effect. The level at which toxicity or other detrimental effects are exhibited by marine organisms is a very hard measure to determine. Different test organisms often show a factor of 100 difference in toxicity to the same contaminant. Further, the organism exhibiting the greatest sensitivity may well be different for different contaminants. Therefore, a sensitivity by some organism to a level of contamination found in a particular environment may not indicate an impairment to the community in that environment if none of the sensitive organisms naturally occur there.

With these uncertainties in mind, Table 4 also lists the lowest of the various "screening" criteria (as compiled by Buchman, 1999). In a general sense, the lowest "screening" criteria may be considered the level of contamination where biological effects may be expected. All the GSB measured averages, and even the maximum measured values, are below the lowest screening level. Clark (2000) noted that the highest levels of cadmium and copper were found near the rivers entering GSB on the opposite side of GSB from Fire Island. In contrast, the values for lead and silver were highest at Fire Island Inlet. This led her to speculate that the major source for these elements may be offshore and related to offshore sewage discharges.

Table 5 shows a comparison between the measured sediment contamination levels from the EPA EMAP station and screening criteria. Some of the metals are near or slightly exceed the lowest screening level. Hence, it is possible that some organisms are negatively impacted at this location. On the other hand, these levels are far below the levels of contamination that one would expect to have a major impact on the majority of the organisms in the system. The assemblage of low and high molecular polycyclic aromatic hydrocarbons (PAH) do not appear to approach levels of concern. Inferences based upon a single station must be made with caution, but given that the station is near the mouth a the Long Island stream, presumably a source of historical contamination, it is reasonable to conclude that the sediments of GSB near Fire Island are likely to be less contaminated and with a lower probability of biological effects from sediment contamination. It should be recognized that the measured compounds do not include many compounds that could possibly be present in harmful concentrations in GSB, such as pesticides. Still the overall picture is that at least the south side of GSB is not likely to be experiencing environmental degradation due to chemical contamination. Additional measurements will have to be made to be certain.

Eutrophication: Nutrients and Oxygen

As an estuary bounded by a heavily populated Long Island, GSB is subject to anthropogenic additions of nutrients, or the process of eutrophication. It is usually the concentrations of the nitrogen fertilizers that stimulate growth of marine plants (i.e., the nitrogen sources are more limiting than phosphorus). Greater nitrogen inputs to a system often result in greater abundances of phytoplankton and macroalgae and can lead to a number of undesirable effects (see for example Nixon, 1995, Hinga et al, 1991, 1995). The amount of chlorophyll-a in water is a measure of phytoplankton abundance. Figure 4 shows a comparison of the average recent levels of total dissolved inorganic nitrogen and chlorphyll-a compared to a few other estuarine systems. GSB appears to have typical chlorophyll abundances and rather low dissolved nitrogen concentrations.

The concentration of nutrients appears to have changed significantly over time in GSB. In contrast to what one might expect from the population growth in the drainage basin of Great South Bay, Clark (2000) found some evidence of decreasing DIN concentrations over time. Her measurements from three surveys in GSB in 1989-1999, when compared to a study in 1979, found that ammonia and urea levels in GSB had decreased, but that nitrate was higher.

More definite trends can be seen in the data from Suffolk County. Figure 5 shows the trend in total dissolved nitrogen (nitrate, nitrite plus ammonia) from the Suffolk County monitoring data. There appears to be a significant downward trend for GSB. The average concentration of DIN appears to have halved in the last 25 years. (The slope of the linear fit is statistically significant at a level of 0.1%, but some caution must be applied as a change in procedures, though none is evident, could have resulted in an apparent slope that is an artifact.) Figures 6 and 7 show the concentrations of ammonia nitrogen and nitrate plus nitrate nitrogen since 1976. The figures show that the decrease in total DIN over time is represented primarily by decreases in ammonia nitrogen over time.

At least part of these trends may be attributed to implementation of sewage management practices that have diverted sewage from individual septic systems and groundwater (which may reach GSB) to an offshore discharge in the Atlantic. The diversion appears to have lowered inputs of nitrogen to GSB. For example, Clark (2000) found that the groundwater concentrations of nitrate at two locations at the northern GSB shore had decreased from 32 μmole/l in 1983 to 2.3 μmole/liter in 1998-1999, and concentrations of nitrogen in rivers entering into GSB had also decreased.

Earlier studies of nutrients in GSB indicated that there is a regular annual cycle of nutrients (e.g., Carpenter et al, 1991). Figures 8 and 9 show the Suffolk County Data for central GSB for all years. There is a general annual pattern of low nitrate plus nitrate values being found most often in late spring through the summer months and higher values in the fall and winter. Presumably, the production of phytoplankton, seagrass, and macroalgae is high in summer and nutrients are readily assimilated by the plants to lower the water column concentrations. However, some low values may be found at any time so there is likely a great deal of variability in the annual pattern of nitrate plus nitrite. Ammonia concentrations show little annual pattern with the exception that the highest values are found in the late fall. Low values may be found at any time. It will require a more extensive analysis than appropriate here to better define the (probably changing) nitrogen dynamics in this system.

Related to the nitrogen dynamics of coastal marine ecosystems is the oxygen dynamics. An issue of concern in many systems is oxygen depletion due to anthropogenic nitrogen inputs. In most marine systems, additions of nitrogen stimulate plant growth. The plant biomass eventually sinks to the bottom of the water column. There, organisms using the plant material to support their metabolism draw down oxygen concentrations in the bottom waters. In some cases oxygen concentrations may be drawn down to essentially zero, making it impossible for organisms (except certain bacteria) to survive. (It also should be noted that when the plants grow, they produce oxygen. If the organisms using the plant material were in the same location as where the plants grew, and used the oxygen before the excess oxygen is lost to the atmosphere, they would use up no more oxygen that originally produced by the plants. However, the plant material is often separated from the produced oxygen by sinking and creates the demand for oxygen at some time, perhaps months later, than when it was produced.)

Figure 10 shows a multi-year record of oxygen concentrations at a station in central GSB. There is a strong seasonal cycle with the oxygen concentrations being highest in late winter and falling to minimum values in late summer. These changes primarily reflect the changing oxygen saturation values due to seasonal temperature variability. There is little difference between surface and bottom oxygen values in most cases. Individual measurements rarely deviate from saturation values by more than 10%. It should be noted that the values shown in Figure 10 are for samples taken in the early morning hours. There is a diurnal oxygen signal in GSB as shown in Figure 11. Oxygen concentrations are highest at the end of the sunlight period (when plants are producing oxygen), and lowest at the end of the nighttime period (due to overnight respiration). As the concentrations shown in Figure 10 are taken in the morning, they represent lower values than would be expected to be found later in the day. With values near saturation levels throughout GSB, oxygen concentrations do not approach hypoxic or anoxic concentrations that would be of concern to organisms. The situation may be different near river mouths at the north side of GSB.

There is one additional feature of GSB that bears note. In her study of the chemistry of GSB, Clark (2000) found that the concentrations of dissolved organic carbon (DOC) in GSB were unusually high. She noted that DOC in GSB exceeded some 98% of the concentrations of DOC measured in two similar mid-Atlantic estuaries. It is not evident what role DOC plays in the nutrient dynamics and ecology of the bay, as DOC appears to have a mostly conservative behavior (i.e., it does not appear to react, degrade or get used by organisms for a food source). Still, there may be minor unidentified components of the bulk DOC which are significant factors in the ecology of the Bay.

Table 2. Monitoring results for fecal coliforms on the ocean side of Fire Island. Max is maximum value found in any sample. N. is number of samples analyzed. Methods are MF = membrane filtration and MPN is most probable number.

Beach	Period	N.	Geometric mean MPN or Colonies per 100 ml	Max.	Method	Source
Robert Moses State Park	1978-1991	181	1.2	16	MF	US EPA via Anon., 1992
"	1992-1993	124	2.6	300	MPN	Suffolk County, 2003
Kismet Beach	1989 &1990		23, 19		MPN	Suffolk County via Anon., 1992
Saltaire Village Beach	1992&1997	19	2.9	220	MPN	Suffolk County, 2003
"	1989 &1990		19, 26		MPN	Suffolk County via Anon., 1992
Great South Beach	1976-1991	180	1.2	45	MF	US EPA via Anon., 1992
Fair Harbor	1993&1996	10	2.5	20	MPN	Suffolk County, 2003
"	1989 &1990		23, 29		MPN	Suffolk County via Anon., 1992
Dunewood Beach	1996	13	1.3	20	MPN	Suffolk County, 2003
"	1989 &1990		19, 32		MPN	Suffolk County via Anon., 1992
Atlantique Beach	1992-1997	42	1.9	140	MPN	Suffolk County, 2003
"	1989 &1990		21, 24		MPN	Suffolk County via Anon., 1992
Ocean Beach	1992-1997	27	1.4	40	MPN	Suffolk County, 2003
"	1989 &1990		21, 24		MPN	Suffolk County via Anon., 1992
Seaview Beach	1992-1997	10	3.3	20	MPN	Suffolk County, 2003
"	1989 &1990		19, 24		MPN	Suffolk County via Anon., 1992
Point O'Woods Beach	1992&1994	21	1.8	40	MPN	Suffolk County, 2003
"	1989 &1990		19, 19		MPN	Suffolk County via Anon., 1992
Sailors Haven	1992-1997	49	2.0	230	MPN	Suffolk County, 2003
"	1989 &1990		19, 45		MPN	Suffolk County via Anon., 1992
"	1984-1988		1.7	80	MF	McNulty, 1989
Cherry Grove	1976-1991	170	1.2	23	MF	US EPA via Anon., 1992
Barrett Beach	1992-1997	42	2.2	16000	MPN	Suffolk County, 2003
"	1989 &1990		19, 23		MPN	Suffolk County via Anon., 1992
Water Island	1976-1991	175	1.2	16	MPN	US EPA via Anon., 1992
Davis Park	1989 &1990		21, 22		MPN	Suffolk County via Anon., 1992
Watch Hill	1992-1997	42	2.0	16000	MPN	Suffolk County, 2003
"	1989 &1990		24, 34		MPN	Suffolk County, 2003
"	1984-1988		1.0	80	MF	McNulty, 1989
Bellport Beach	1976-1991	165	1.3	26	MF	US EPA via Anon., 1992
"	1992-1997	26	2.6	1300	MPN	Suffolk County, 2003
"	1989 &1990		39,32		MPN	Suffolk County via Anon., 1992
Smith Point County Park	1976-1991	167	1.3	64	MF	US EPA via Anon., 1992
"	1993-1994	31	2.4	110	MPN	Suffolk County, 2003
Moriches Inlet	1976-1991	160	1.4	168	MF	US EPA via Anon 1992

Table 3. Monitoring results for fecal coliforms on the bay side of Fire Island.

Beach	Period	N	Geometric mean MPN or Colonies per 100 ml	Max.	Method	Source
Saltaire Village Beach (Bay)	1989 &1990		19, 51		MPN	Suffolk County via Anon., 1992
	1993-1996	26	2.8		MPN	Suffolk County, 2003
Fair Harbor (Bay)	1989 & 1990		43, 116		MPN	Suffolk County via Anon., 1992
Atlantique Beach (Bay)	1989 & 1990		452, 192		MPN	Suffolk County via Anon., 1992
	1992-1997	39	53.3	2400	MPN	Suffolk County, 2003
Ocean Beach (Bay)	1989 & 1990		35, 84		MPN	Suffolk County via Anon., 1992
	1992-1996	23	15.9	700	MPN	Suffolk County, 2003
Ocean Beach STP outfall	1979-2002	57	2.0	1900	MPN	Suffolk County, 2003
Seaview Beach (Bay)	1989 & 1990		48, 264		MPN	Suffolk County via Anon., 1992
	1992-1996	20	3.8	500	MPN	Suffolk County, 2003
Club at Point O'Woods Beach (Bay)	1989 & 1990		142, 41		MPN	Suffolk County via Anon., 1992
	1992&1994	18	4.6		MPN	Suffolk County, 2003
Sailors Haven Marina	1984-1988	80	16.2		MF	McNulty, 1989
Sailors Haven Buoy	1984-1988	80	1.2		MF	McNulty, 1989
Talisman (boating area)	1984-1988	80	5.4		MF	McNulty, 1989
Barrett Beach	1996-1997	21	8.7	3000	MPN	Suffolk County, 2003
Watch Hill Beach	1996	11	24.9	800	MPN	Suffolk County, 2003
Watch Hill Marina	1984-1988	80	60.9		MF	McNulty, 1989
Watch Hill Buoy	1984-1988	80	0.5		MF	McNulty, 1989
Bellport Beach	1996	9	4.4	300	MPN	Suffolk County, 2003
Old Inlet	1984-1988	80	3		MF	McNulty, 1989
Boat channel at Smith Point (Sta 090100)	1976-2002	82	9.5	600	MPN	Suffolk County, 2003
Central Great South Bay north of Tailsman (Sta. 090150)	1984-1988	80	0.7		MF	McNulty, 1989
GSB off Davis Park (Sta 090140)	1976-2002	64	1.7	80	MPN	Suffolk County, 2003
Centraol GSB north of Point O'Woods (Sta 090170)	1976-2002	209	1.9	280	MPN	Suffolk County, 2003

Table 4. Concentrations of trace metals in the surface water of Great South Bay compared to NOAA screening levels. Average values are the averages of 25 to 28 measurements from Clark (2000) and are based upon 8 to 10 stations in GSB measured in September 1998, April 1999, and August, 1999. The screening values listed are the lowest of the marine values indicated in the NOAA SQuiRT tables (Buchman, 1999). All values in μg/liter

Metal	Average	Maximum	Lowest screening level
Silver	0.0031	0.0062	0.95
Lead	0.056	0.2	8.1
Copper	0.98	1.65	3.1
Chromium	0.025	0.18	9.3

Table 5. Measures of sediment contaminants from an EPA EMAP station (Station VA-023), approximately 500 meters off the mouth of the Swan River in northeast GSB. Sample date was August 19, 1990. Screening levels are the lowest value given for any of the marine sediment screening levels for each chemical in the NOAA SQuiRT tables (Buchman, 1999)

Element or chemical	Measured value	Lowest screening value	Units
Antimony	0.4	9.3	ug/g
Arsenic	5.4	7.24	ug/g
Cadmium	0.5	0.676	ug/g
Chromium	29.9	52.3	ug/g
Copper	20.6	18.7	ug/g
Lead	45.3	30.24	ug/g
Mercury	0.16	0.13	ug/g
Nickel	12.3	15.9	ug/g
Selenium	0.38	1	ug/g
Silver	<1	0.73	ug/g
Tin	6.02	3.4	ug/g
Zinc	104	124	ug/g
1-methylnaphthalene	2.27		ng/g
1-methylphenanthrene	1.14		ng/g
2,3,5-trimethylnaphthalene	<43.5		ng/g
2,6-dimethylnaphthalene	<45.8		ng/g
2-methylnaphthalene	<47.4	20	ng/g
Acenaphthene	1.14	6.7	ng/g
Acenaphthlylene	1.14	5.9	ng/g
Anthracene	1.14	47	ng/g
Biphenyl	1.14		ng/g
Fluorene	2.27	19	ng/g
Naphthalene	9.08	35	ng/g
Phenanthrene	20.4	87	ng/g
Low Molecular Weight PAHs	17	312	ng/g
Benz(a)anthracene	25	75	ng/g
Benzo(a)pyrene	1.14	89	ng/g
Benzo(b+k)fluoranthene	52.2	1800	ng/g
Benzo(e)pyrene	22.7	89	ng/g
Benzo(g,h,i)perylene	<64.6	670	ng/g
Chrysene	26.1	107	ng/g
Dibenz(a,h)anthracene	<50.1	6	ng/g
Fluoranthene	44.3	600	ng/g
Indeno(1,2,3-c,d)pyrene	<49.6	600	ng/g
Perylene	5.68		ng/g
Pyrene	43.1	665	ng/g
High Molecular Weight PAHs	243	1700	ng/g
TOTAL PAHS	260	4022	ng/g
Dibutyltin	<4		ng/g

Element or chemical	Measured value	Lowest screening value	Units
monobutyltin	<10		ng/g
Tributyltin	<4		ng/g

Figure 4. Comparison of GSB annual average dissolved inorganic nitrogen concentrations (DIN) and chlorophyll (CHL) concentrations to other coastal systems. The systems are: 1) Great South Bay; 2) Kaneohe Bay; 3) Chesapeake Bay main stem; 4) Narragansett Bay; 5) Patuxent River Estuary; 6) Delaware Bay; 7) Potomac River Estuary; 8) Apalachicola Bay; 9) Pamlico Bay; 10) South San Francisco Bay, 12) Barataria Bay; 13) North San Francisco Bay; 14) Mobile Bay; 16) New York Harbor. Chlorophyll data are the average values for station 090170 from Suffolk County for 1993-2000. DIN concentrations are averages from three bay-wide surveys by Clark (2000) in 1998 and 1999. Data for other estuaries were provided by S. Nixon and M. Pilson, Personal Communication, 1994. It should be noted that data for the other estuaries are typically from the 1980s and the current situation in those systems may be different.

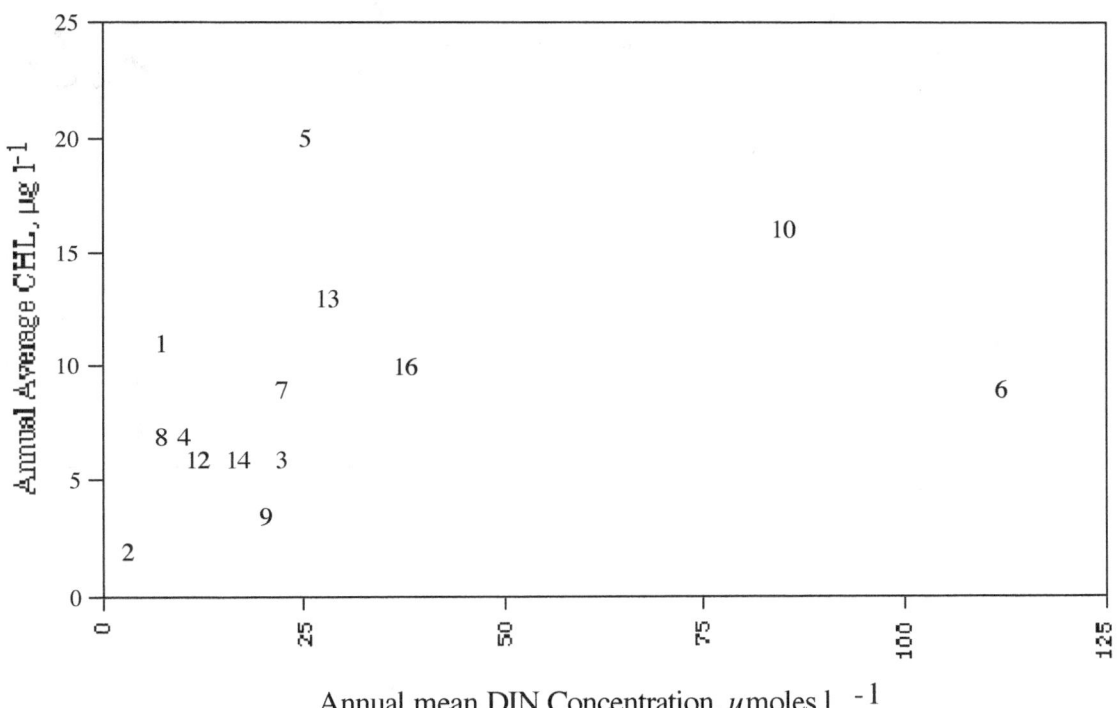

Figure 5. DIN Concentrations over time at station 090170. Line is linear regression fits to the data.

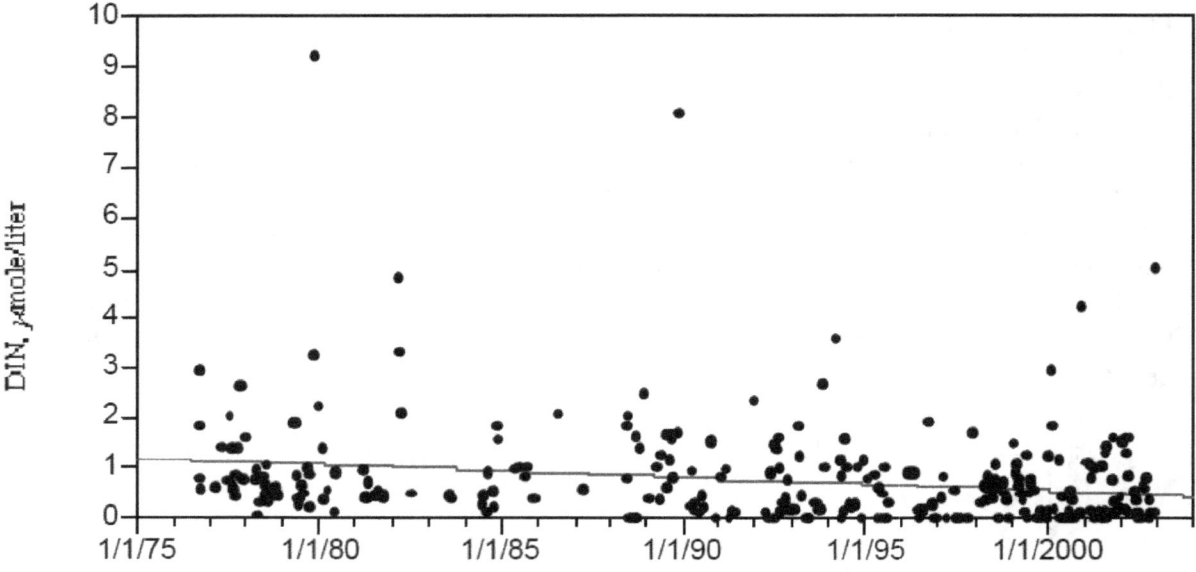

Figure 6. Concentrations of nitrate plus nitrite over time at station 090170. Line is a linear regression to the data.

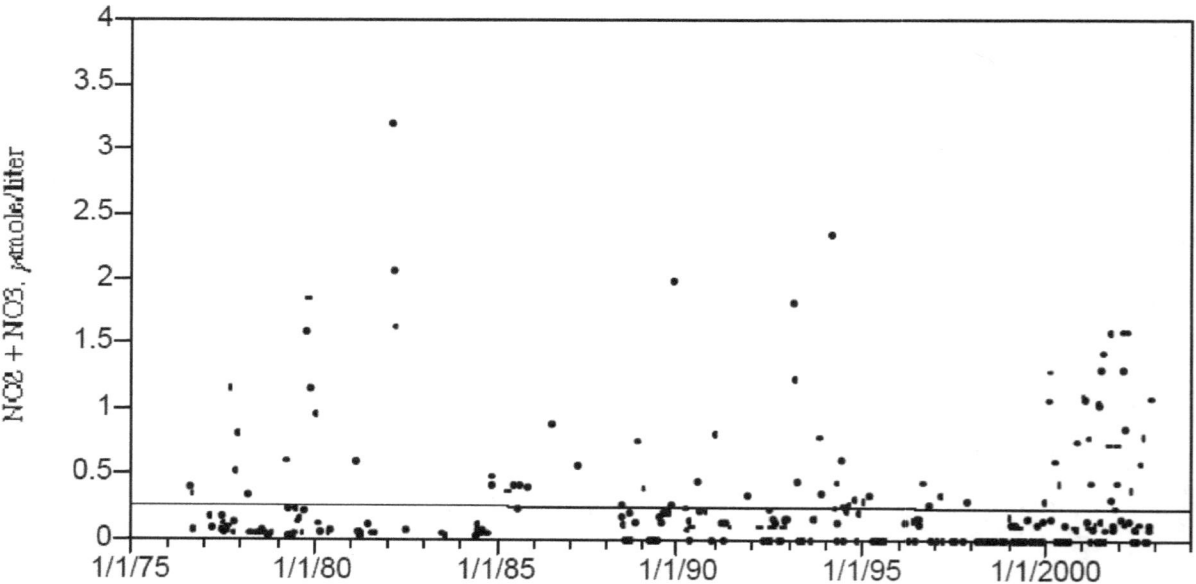

Figure 7. Concentration of ammonia nitrogen over time. Line is a linear regression fit to the data.

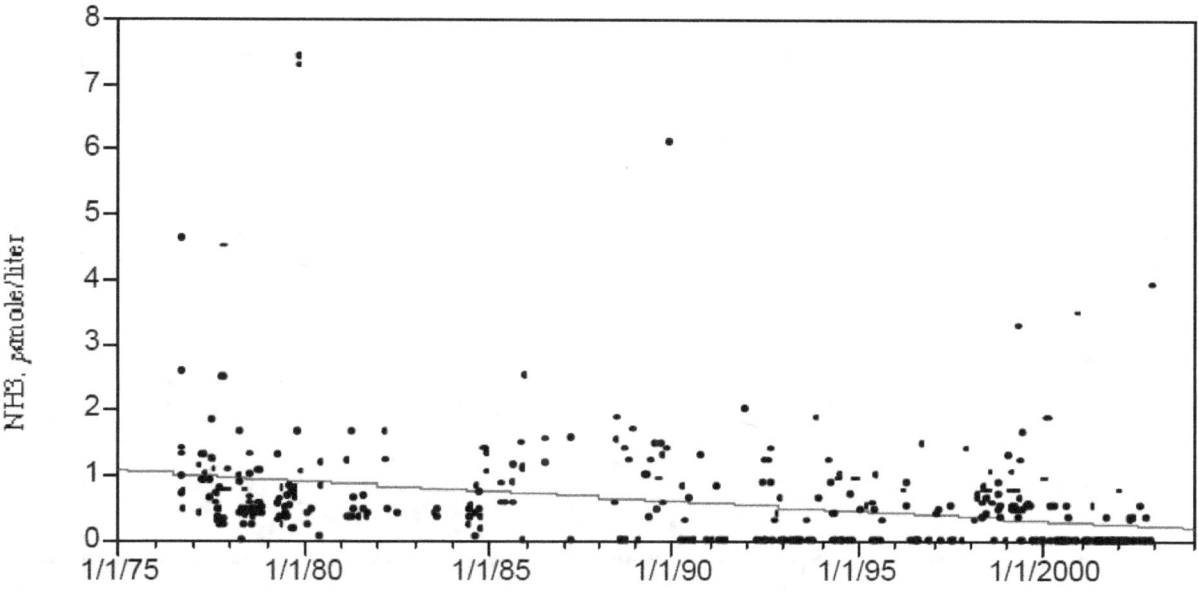

Figure 8. Nitrate plus nitrite concentrations at station 090170 from all years.

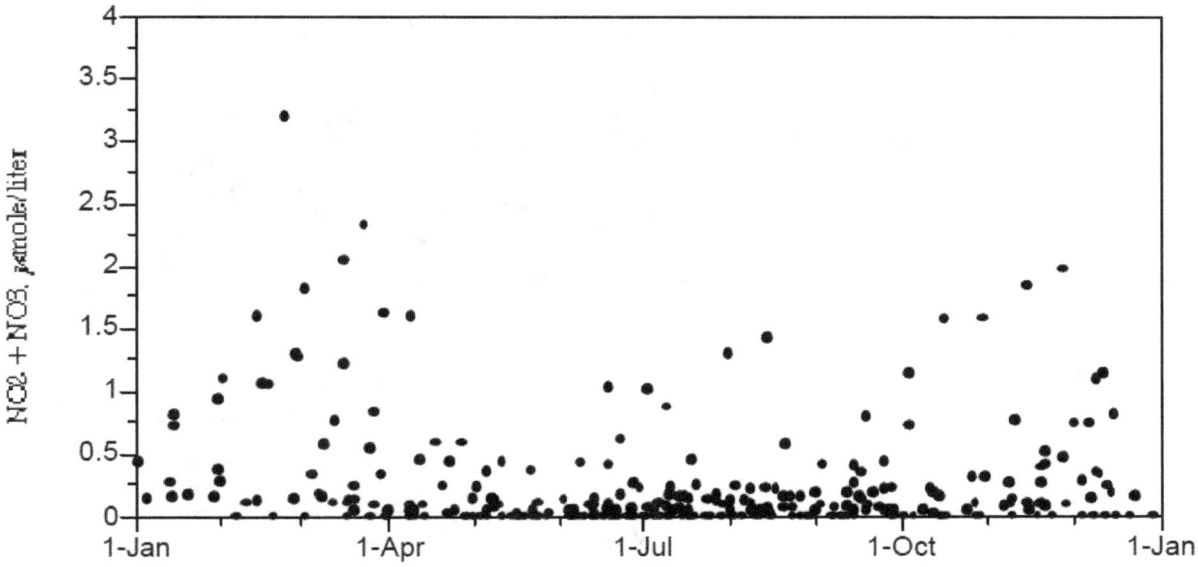

Figure 9. Ammonia concentrations at station 090170 from all years. Two high values of 6 and 7 μmole/liter have been omitted (November values) to put figure on same scale as prior figure.

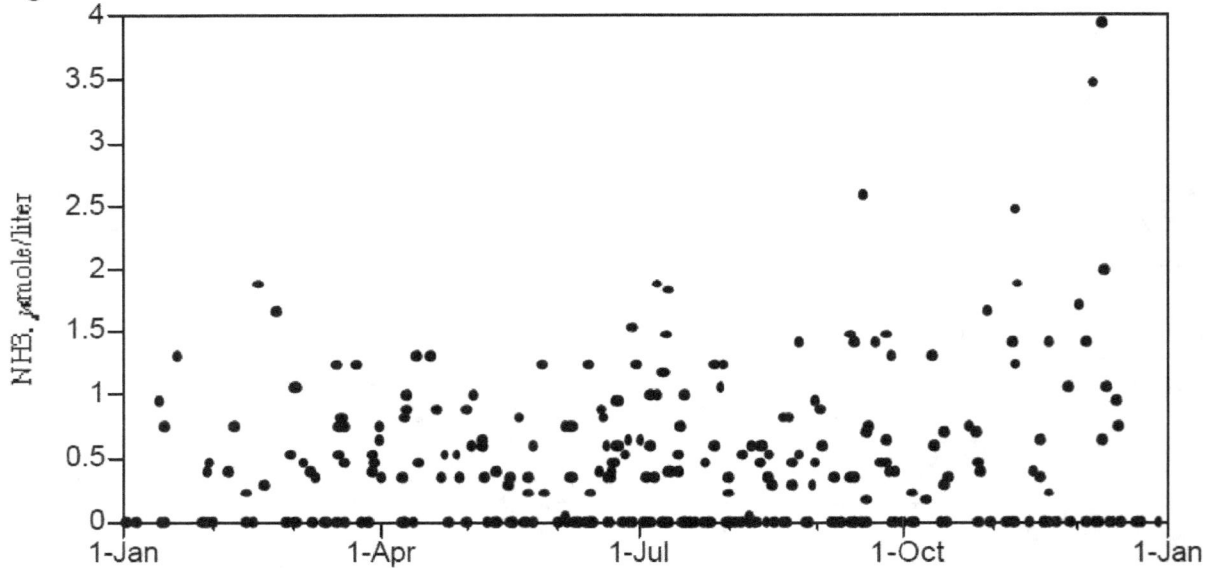

Figure 10. Surface and bottom oxygen concentrations in central GSB. Samples are taken in the morning.

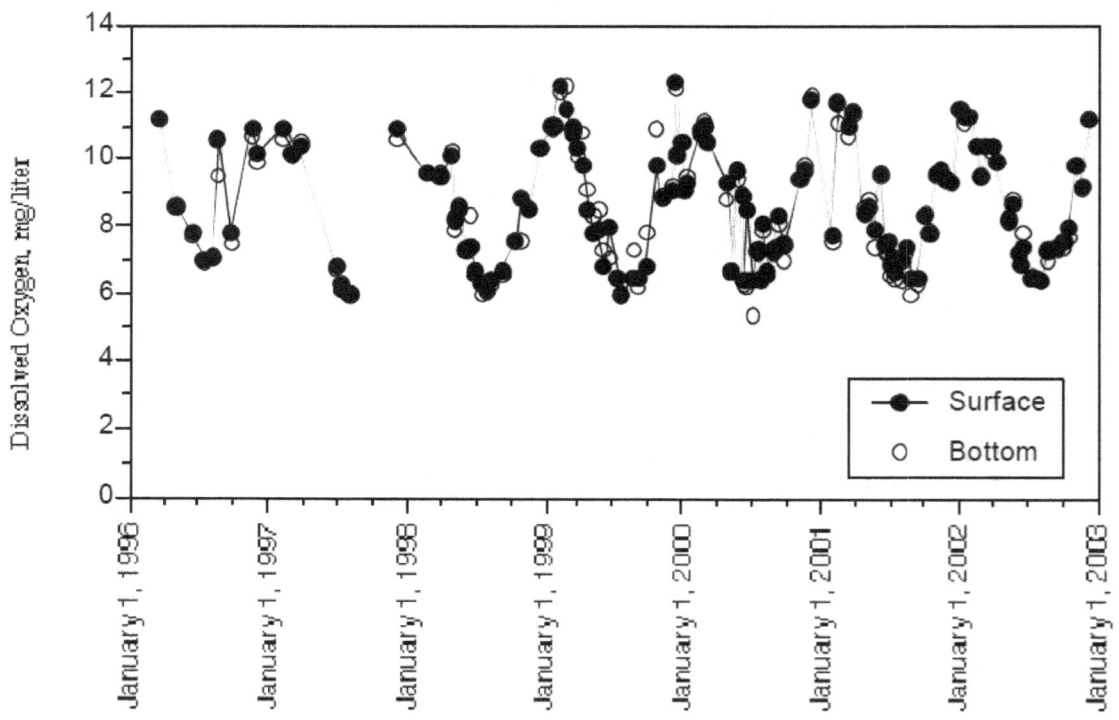

Figure 11. Diurnal oxygen concentrations at stations in GSB. Data is from Suffolk County, 1993. The diurnal measurements were conducted on September 17 to 19, 1976.

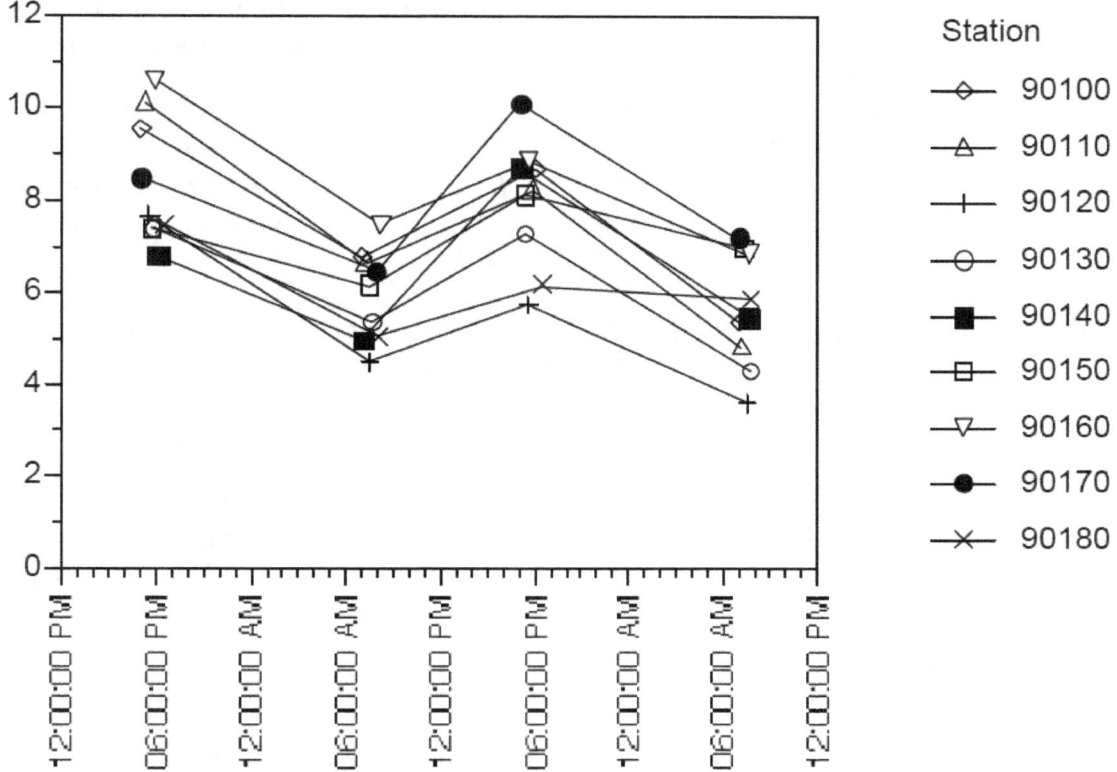

Diurnal oxygen concentrations

BIOLOGICAL RESOURCES

Primary Production and Plant Abundance

The Great South Bay has been known as a coastal ecosystem with one of the greatest rates of primary production (plant growth) ever measured (Carpenter et al., 1991). The total primary production for GSB is comprised of phytoplankton production, seagrass production, macroalgae production and salt marsh production. Lively et al. (1983) estimated the phytoplankton production to be 450 g $C/m^2/yr$. Carpenter gave an estimate for average eelgrass production of 70 g $C/m^2/yr$ that totaled 520 g $C/m^2/yr$. This estimate does not include the production of fringing salt marshes or from marcoalgae that may produce additional carbon. Even without the additional unknown inputs, GSB produced as much plant growth per unit area as an intensely cultivated agricultural plot (Carpenter et al., 1991).

Lively et al. (1983) reported that the phytoplankton standing stock for the GSB had an annual cycle with highest abundances in the summer months. That pattern still appears to be the case as is shown in Figure 12. While there is a considerable year to year variability, high standing stocks of phytoplankton chlorophyll are usually found from late June through October. The minimum values tend to occur in the spring months.

There appear to be no recent studies of primary production in GSB, but there are indications that the primary production may be decreasing. As noted earlier, the levels of dissolved nitrogen in GSB have decreased over the last 25 years. The average standing stock of phytoplankton chlorophyll has decreased by about 30% in central GSB over the last 15 years (Figure 13.)

The decrease in phytoplankton chlorophyll does not necessarily mean that the total primary production has decreased. The standing stock of phytoplankton is an abundance measure, not a measure of the rate of production. Even if decreasing phytoplankton chlorophyll is an indicator of decreasing phytoplankton production, there may be a compensating increase in seagrass production so the total primary production may not have decreased. What is clear however, is that with a decrease in abundance of phytoplankton stocks, the herbivores (such as the hard clam) that depend on phytoplankton may not be as well nourished as at prior times. At the very least, herbivores will have to expend more effort to harvest the same amount of phytoplankton.

Brown Tides

Since the summer of 1985, a marine phytoplankton organism, *Aureococcus anophagefferens*, popularly called the brown tide, has bloomed periodically to disruptive levels in GSB. *A. anophagefferns* is a very poor nutrition source for most herbivores. During very large brown tide blooms, *A. anophagefferns* becomes nearly the only phytoplankton species present. Further, the presence of *A. anophagefferns* appears to mechanically interfere with the ingestion of other types of phytoplankton, essentially starving the herbivore when brown tides occur. Herbivore species such as the hard clam, *Mercenaria mercenaria*, once the primary commercial harvest of GSB, can experience significant (e.g., 67%) mortalities during brown tide blooms and those that do survive may not grow during the bloom at all (Greenfield and Lonsdale, 2002). Another consequence of brown tide blooms is damage to sea grasses. The brown tide blooms are dense enough to prevent light sufficient to support the growth of sea grasses to reach the bottom (Bricelj, 1996, McElroy, 1996).

In 1985, *A. anophagefferns* occurred in bloom concentrations in a number of embayments in the northeast US. Since that time, recurrent large blooms of *A. anophagefferns* have only occurred in GSB and the Peconic Bays. Brown tide blooms have occurred roughly every other year in GSB as is shown in Figure 14 for three stations in central GSB. It should be noted that the bloom levels within GSB are patchy within the Bay reaching different maximum concentrations in different areas. An alternate view of the data in Figure 14 on a logarithmic scale, shows that *A. anophageffern* is present at most times at low concentrations, with only a relatively few samples being below the detection limit of the counts.

The reasons for the first widespread blooms in 1985, the persistence of brown tide blooms in GSB and the Peconic Bays and the year to year variability remain unresolved. It is clear that *A. anophagefferns* blooms are not caused by simple additions of inorganic nitrogen nutrients (Keller and Rice, 1989; Nixon et al., 1994; Gobler et al., 2002). It seems likely that the proximal cause of brown tide blooms is related to the relatively high levels of dissolved organic matter found in GSB (Clark, 2000), and the ability of *A. anophagefferns* to make use of the dissolved organic carbon and possibly organic nitrogen sources (Lomas et al., 2001; Gobler and Sanudo-Wilhelmy, 2001;Gobler et al., 2002; Mulholland et al., 2002).

Until the brown tide phenomenon recedes in GSB, its recurrence will continue to have impacts on the GSB ecosystem, particularly the shellfish organisms suitable for commercial harvest.

Figure 12. Chlorophyll abundances at four stations in GSB. Data is from Suffolk County, 1993 and covers the years 1988 to 2002.

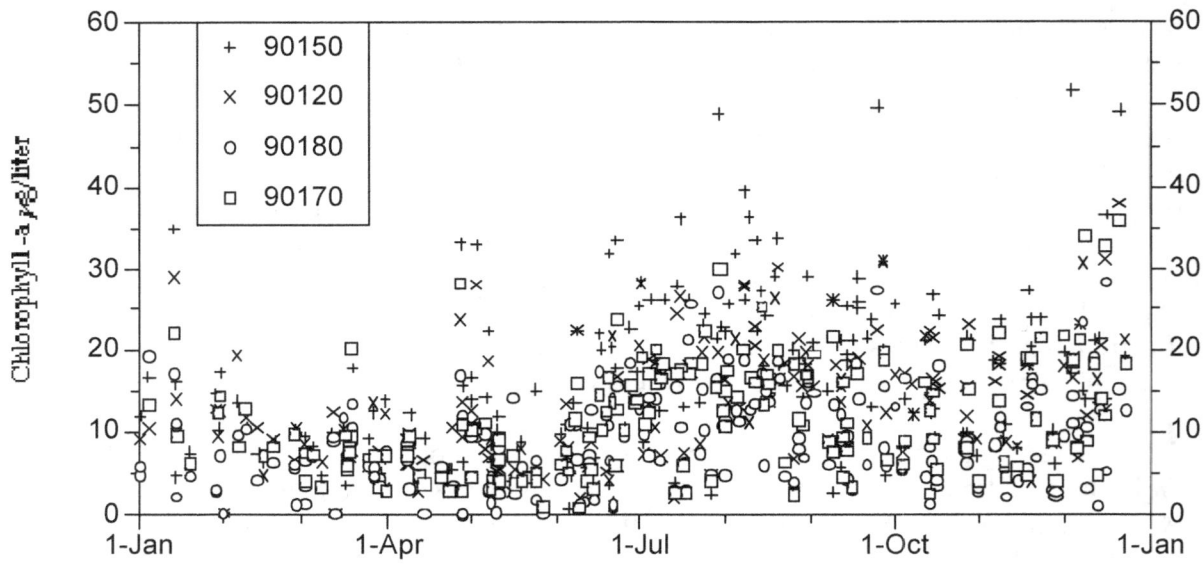

Figure 13. Chlorophyll abundance over time at four stations in central GSB. Data is from Suffolk County, 1993. The lines are linear regression fits to each station.

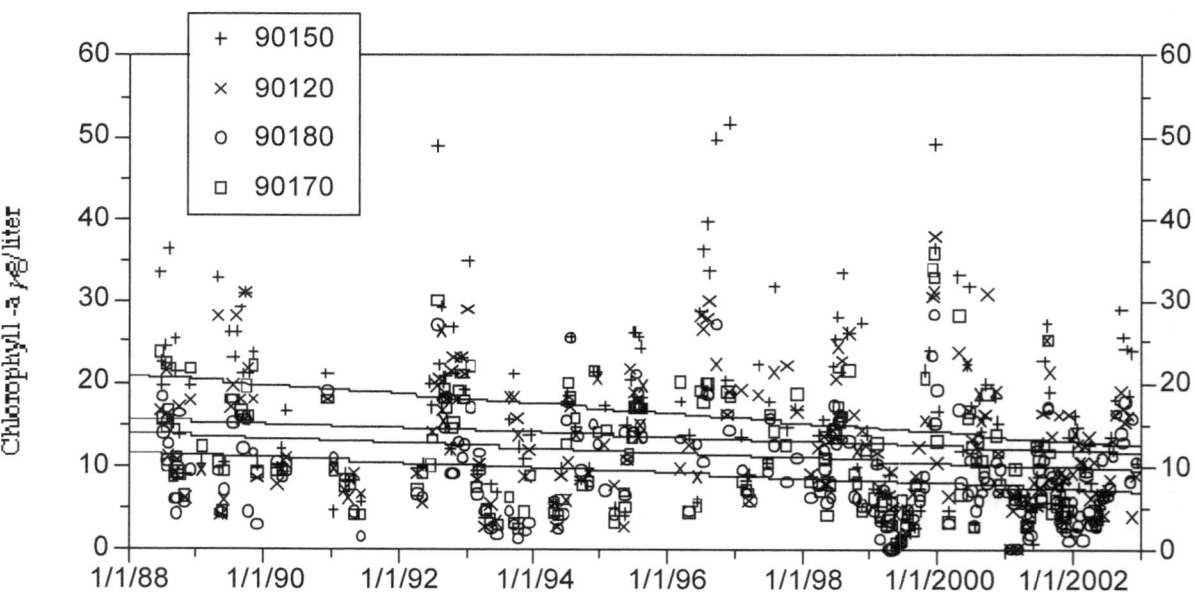

Figure 14. Abundance of the brown tide phytoplankton, *Aureococcus anophagefferns*, at three stations in Great South Bay. Data is from Suffolk County, 2003.

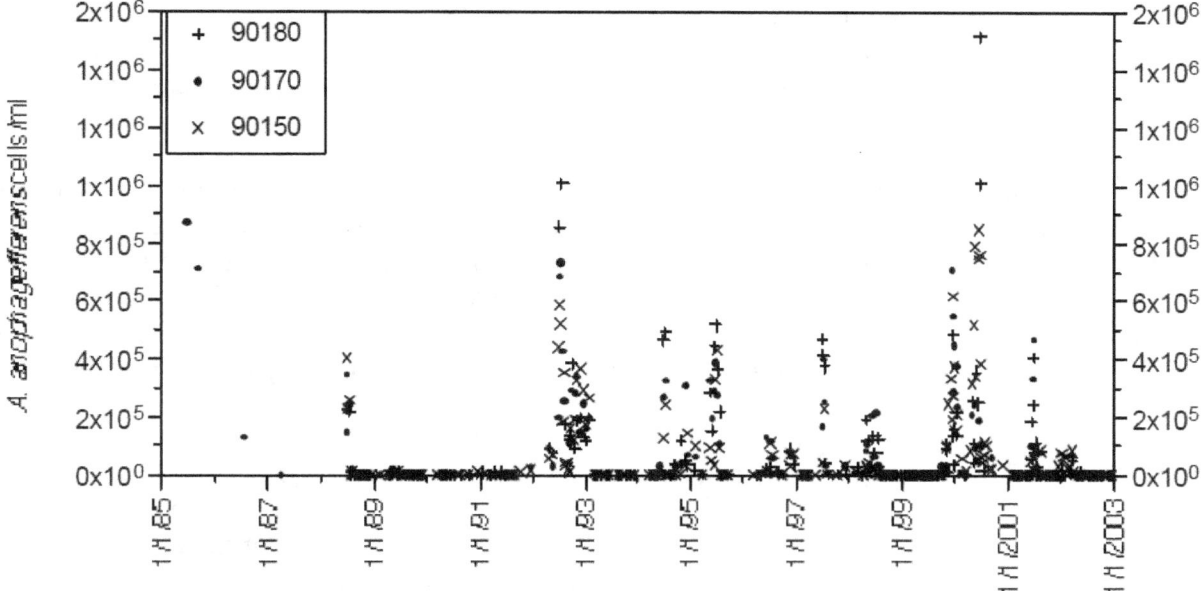

Figure 15. Same as Figure 14 but with a logarithmic scale to illustrate the distribution of low concentrations of cells. Data observations listed as zero or less than a detection limit were plotted as 1 cell/ml.

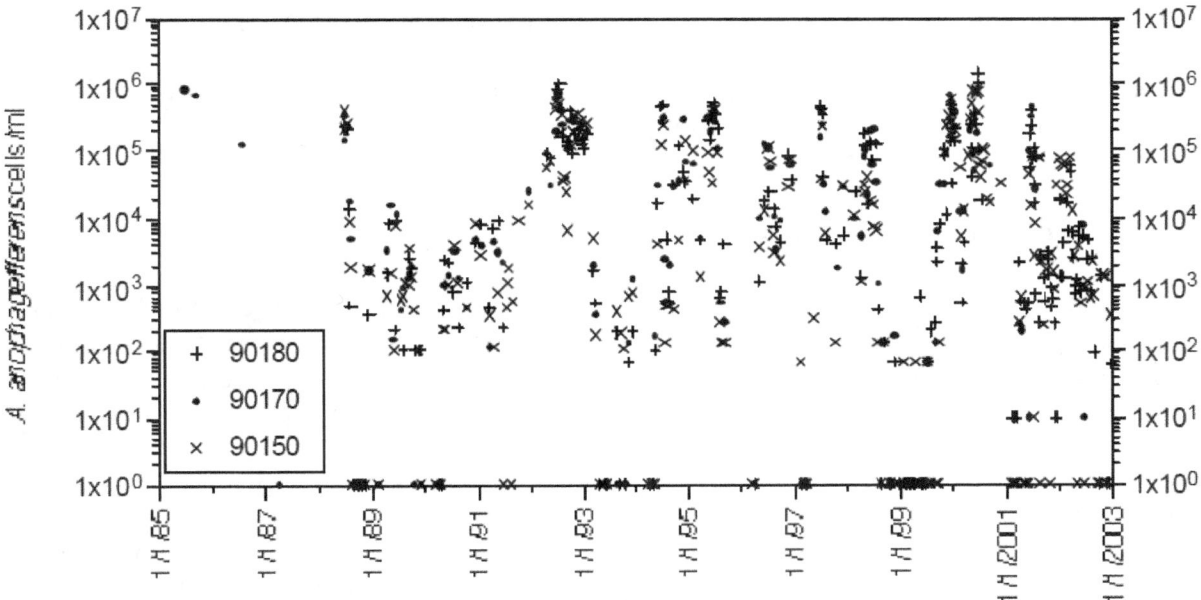

BENTHIC HABITAT TYPES

The benthos of GSB may be divided into four major types of habitats:
1) areas covered by submerged aquatic vegetation, especially seagrasses
2) unvegetated areas of sandy or muddy sediments
3) intertidal sandy beaches
4) salt marshes (An examination of GSB salt marshes will be covered in another background report.)

There is scant information on the biota in intertidal beaches, with the exception of the one relevant thesis on ocean-side beaches by Steinback (1999). Among other observations, she found that there was a difference between the fauna in communities inhabiting beaches with high and low off-road vehicle traffic. It appears that the effect of vehicles is largely to disperse and dry out the wrack (a source of food and habitat for organisms). She also noted however, that the effects of vehicle disturbance were small in comparison to the effects of a large storm.

There is often a theme in marine management literature regarding the values of certain types of habitat. It should be recognized that these are values judged by human needs and desires, and not based upon some intrinsic value or goodness to the functioning of the planet as habitat for earth's life. All four of the types of habitat in GSB offer valuable habitat, just different types of habitat. For example, eelgrass beds are often touted as valuable habitat for scallops, shrimp, and many types of juvenile fish. Certainly that is not the case for all fish. The bay anchovy, for example, appears to survive better in unvegetated areas of GSB than in seagrass beds (Castro, 1990). Unvegetated areas of GSB are the primary habitat of the adult hard clam, *Merceneria Mercenaria,* which supported major commercial fisheries in GSB for decades.

Sometimes an economic-political decision is made to maximize a particular resource to the benefit of some user group. One such example is creation of the Kismet and Fisherman's artificial reefs in GSB. These were created to provide new fishing and diving resources by changing the type of habitat. Kismet reef was constructed of some 4,000 tires, two barges, 24,000 cement blocks, and concrete rubble.

Submerged Aquatic Vegetation

There appears to be little systematic study of the abundance or distribution of submerged vascular plants or of macroalgae in GSB in recent years. The vascular plant eelgrass, *Zostra marina*, is thought to be good nursery habitat for many species. Eelgrass beds also provide habitat for many small species of fish that are prey for desirable species of sport fish (Pohle et al., 1991).

Like other biota in GSB, the abundance of eelgrass has varied greatly over time (Carpenter et al, 1991). Eelgrass nearly disappeared from the Bay in the mid 1930s, as it did through much of the northeast US coastal waters due to wasting disease (Short et al., 1987). This loss apparently led to, or contributed to, the reduction of some desirable species including bay scallops, shrimps, and oysters. By the mid 1960s, eelgrass had recovered and reached dense growths, with the consequence that some boaters thought the grasses were at nuisance level as the grasses sometimes fouled propellers. There were a number of reports of eelgrass densities as great as 2 to 4.5 kg/m^2 (Carpenter et al., 1991). The levels of eelgrass appeared stable through the 1970s. During that period, the maximum depth of occurrence of eelgrass was stated to be 1.8 m on the south side of the GSB and 0.5 m on the north side. The depth restriction on the northern side was due to a greater turbidity on the north side of GSB and the resultant lack of light penetration needed to support eelgrass growth. An aerial survey during the summer of 1981 provided a map of the distribution of eelgrass, provided in Carpenter et al. (1991). It was estimated that eelgrass covered one third of the Bay. The densest eelgrass beds were along the south side of the Bay, especially at the eastern end of Fire Island and off East and West Fire Islands. This distribution largely coincides with the shallowest portions of GSB, thus it may be concluded that the eelgrass occurs where the water is shallow enough to allow sufficient light penetration.

The onset of the brown tide events has caused a significant reduction in light penetration during major bloom periods with a resultant reduction in eelgrass leaf density in GSB (Cosper et al., 1987). The net impact on the distribution and abundance of eelgrass of the irregular brown tide blooms over the last 15 years do not appear to have been systematically quantified.

However, one limited comparison can be made. Green et al. (1977) found eelgrass beds in eastern GSB to have an average biomass of 200 g/m^2. In their study of the nekton associated with eelgrass beds adjacent to Fire Island, Raposa and Oviatt (2000) found beds adjacent to bay-side beaches to have densities of about 120 g/m^2 and beds adjacent to salt marshes to have densities of about 40 g/m^2. There was considerable variability between their study sites, and these are not the same sites studied by Green et al (1977), so the apparent reduction in eelgrass biomass must be viewed with some caution.

The Raposa and Oviatt (2000) study also provides some insight into the biomass of macroalgae found in GSB. At the beach eelgrass sites, macroalgae was found at 1 g/m^2 or less. At the marsh eelgrass sites, macroalgae could be found at maximum densities (in July) of 20 g/m^2.

Unvegetated Benthos: Hard Clam Habitat

Most of the interest in the sandy and muddy unvegetated benthos is as habitat for the hard clam, *M. merceneria*. The hard clam has a special place in the history of GSB and its peoples. Hard clams were the mainstay of an important commercial fishery and the colorful baymen who harvested the clams (see Kassner and Squires 1991; McHugh, 1991). Due to the value of the commercial harvest of hard clams, even at its current low state, hard clam abundance and its relationship to habitat characteristics has been investigated relatively often (Wallace, 1991; Kassner, 1991; Ward, 1993; Papa, 1994; Larson, 2000, and Maher and Cerrato, 2000). Much of the interest has been in determining the relationship between clam abundance, recruitment, and growth with environmental parameters. One motivation is to find a practice that would lead to greater clam abundance and commercial harvests.

Hard clams in GSB are found in quite variable abundance. Irregular patches of high abundance may have 13.5 hard clams per square meter (with some reports of 19 hard clams per square meter) while the average of lower density areas are about 2 clams per square meter. The overall average is about 6 clams per square meter. The transition between low and high abundance areas can occur over short distances. Kassner et al. (1991) noted that the abundance of four-year-old clams was the same in high and low abundance areas, but that the abundance of young clams was an order of magnitude higher in the high abundance areas. Expressed differently, clams grow best where clams have already grown in high abundances.

Wallace (1991) compared hard clam density estimates to earlier studies in the 1970s and concluded that the total abundance of hard clams has not declined, even though the harvest has declined dramatically. What had changed was that there has been a shift in size and age structure to smaller, younger individuals in the population. In contrast, Maher and Cerrato (2000) citing annual clam census data from the town of Brookhaven (begun in 1986) state that the overall clam population is "in decline." The difference in conclusions may represent the difference in time periods considered.

High abundances of hard clams are associated with specific sediment characteristics. High abundances of clams are found in sediments with a larger fraction of course-grained materials, especially shell fragments (Maher and Cerrato, 2000). Shell hash areas appear to provide a beneficial habitat for hard clams that also supports a more diverse community of suspension feeders and carnivores (Larson, 2000). Experimental results indicated that clams grew faster in shell hash, and that mud crabs (a clam predator) spent little time in shell hash (Larson, 2000).

The towns of Brookhaven and Islip have management authority over shellfish. The towns practice stock augmentation and have sponsored studies to see if there are ways to increase the harvest, but there appears to be no report of the success of any program to increase harvests.

Commercial and Recreational Harvests

The Great South Bay has supported important fisheries since records were first kept in 1880 (McHugh, 1991). Landings records are often used as a surrogate for abundance estimates for a particular species or population. It should be recognized that landing records are actually a measure of marketability, consumer preference, harvest effort, natural abundance, and the conventions and diligence of record keepers. Landings records are at best an imperfect measure of abundance of a population. With that qualifier, the recent history of landings for a number of species is available from records kept by the National Marine Fisheries Service. In most years, the landing records for New York State include a location code for the area fished. The landings identified for Great South Bay are used here.

Commercial landings data also do not capture the recreational fishery. For many species, especially many of the popular finfish, the recreational capture may be substantial and even exceed the commercial landings. The recreational harvesting of many shellfish, which takes little capital investment may also be significant. Recreational harvests are very difficult to estimate, and there do not appear to be any recent attempts to quantify recreational catches.

Hard Clams and Other Bivalve Mollusks

During the late 1800s through about 1930, GSB was known for its oyster production. Hard clams, also called quahogs, probably were also in abundance during this time, but there was a market preference for oysters. There was considerable oyster culture through 1930 to supply the market demand (Schubel et al, 1991). A shortage of red meat toward the end of World War II caused GSB hard clam landings to increase sharply to over 10 million pounds in 1947 (McHugh, 1991). Landings dropped off nearly as sharply to a low of just over 2 million pounds in 1954. Hard clam harvests reached another peak in the mid 1970s of about 9 million pounds and have been falling since (Figure 16). In 2001, the NMFS estimated the harvest of hard clams from GSB to have a market value of $1,471,156. While this value is considerably reduced from earlier years, the hard clam landings still represent a major proportion of the commercial fishery in GSB. In 2000 and 2001, clams accounted for 95% and 98% of the value of commercial harvest for GSB, respectively.

The importance of the hard clam harvest can be seen in the NMFS-estimated total dollar value for all species in the commercial harvest (Figure 17). The harvest of other species has not increased to make up for the decline in the hard clam harvest.

Oysters (*Crassostrea virginicus*), soft shell clams (*Mya arenaria*), and blue mussel (*Mytilus edulis*) are also reported in the commercial harvest from GSB. These species appear to have quite variable landings marked by an occasional year with landings as much as ten times its typical landing (Figure 18).

Crustacea

A variety of crab species may be found in GSB. These include the blue crab (*Callinedtes sapidus*), Jonah crab (*Cancer borealis*), rock crab (*Cancer irroratus*), lady crab (*Ovalipes ocellatus*), fiddler crab (*Uca pugnax*), green crab (*Carcinus maenas*), spider crab (*Libinia emarginata*), and mud crab (*Neopanope texana*). The horseshoe crab (*Limulus polyphemus*) is found in GSB, but is a crab in name only being an Aracanid. Even though not commercially harvested, some of the crab species are important components of the ecosystem as predators and prey. For example, the blue, mud, stone, and green crabs are predators on hard clams, especially juvenile clams.

The blue crab is a common and edible species and the major harvestable crab in GSB. There has long been a recreational catch for the blue and rock crabs, but these were never a major component of the commercial catch. The blue crab is near the northern limit of its range in

GSB and is subject to dieoff in cold winters. Reports of a fishery for blue crabs in GSB go back to the early 1900s, but the blue crab was not a significant component of the commercial fishery through much of the century. However, in the 1990s the commercial landings of blue crabs rose sharply to unprecedented levels (Figure 19), only to drop off again to low levels.

Even at its maximum harvest years in 1993 and 1996, blue crab landings were still valued at only 12 to 25% of the value of hard clam landings. Without additional information, it is not possible to determine if the blue crab population increased during this period. It may be that the pulse of landings represents an increase in fishing effort, perhaps in part due to the reduction in clam landings. If that is the case, it would appear that the increased fishing effort was not sustainable and soon depleted the crab population.

The American lobster has only been listed once in the 1981 - 2002 commercial harvest with a grand total of just four pounds of harvest.

Finfish

The National Marine Fisheries Service database for GSB since 1981 includes the following species of finfish that are reported in commercial landings: stripped bass, bluefish, bonito, butterfish, American eel, winter flounder, summer flounder, goosefish, silver hake, king whiting, launces, mackerel, menhaden, white perch, puffers, scups, sea bass, searobins, shad, dogfish sharks, shad, silversides, skates, sturgeons, albacore tuna, tautog, and weakfish. Many of these species only occur in the landings records for one or two years while others are erroneously placed among GSB landings (e.g. Albacore Tuna). Only a few species show up regularly in the commercial landings. Figure 20 shows the landings for two of the species more regularly found in the record, bluefish and weakfish. The landings are quite variable with an occasional exceptional year of very high landings.

As noted earlier, many of the finfishes are probably subject to a greater take by recreational than commercial fishing. Saltwater recreational fishing is a major recreational activity that in addition to the recreation itself provides economic benefits to the state from the fishing support commercial sector.

Figure 16. Hard clam harvest from GSB since 1981. Data is from National Marine Fisheries Service, 2003. No data for GSB is available for the years 1986 to 1988, as the landings for New York State were not given location codes.

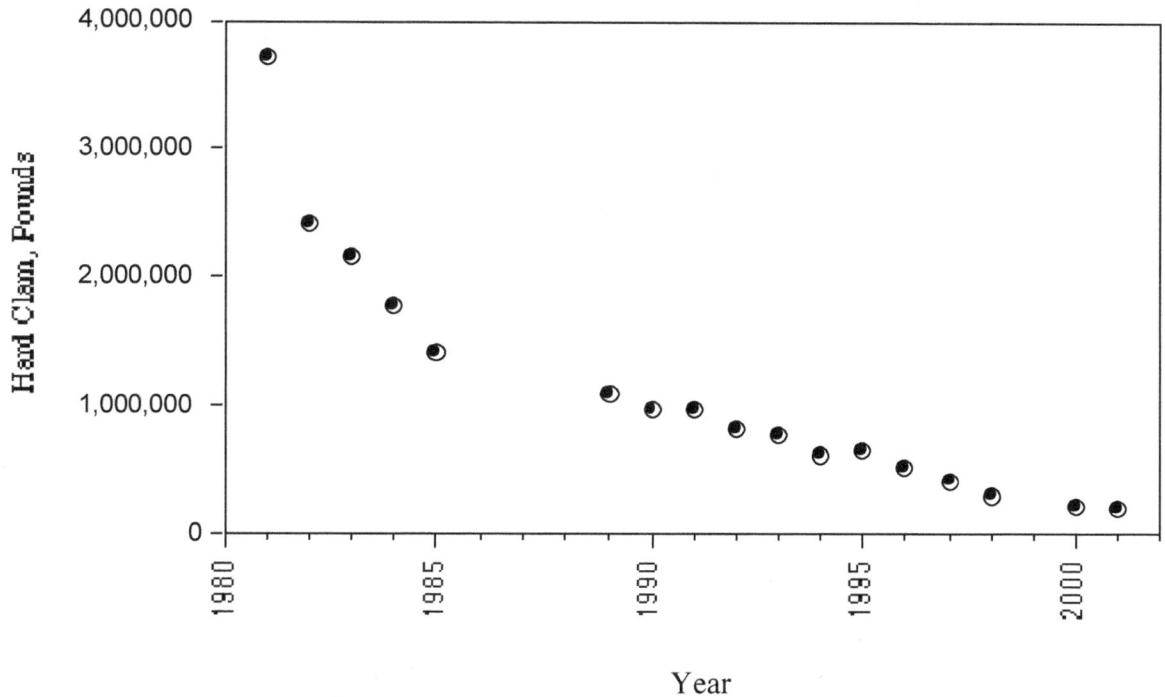

Figure 17. Total dollar value of commercial landings of all species from Great South Bay.

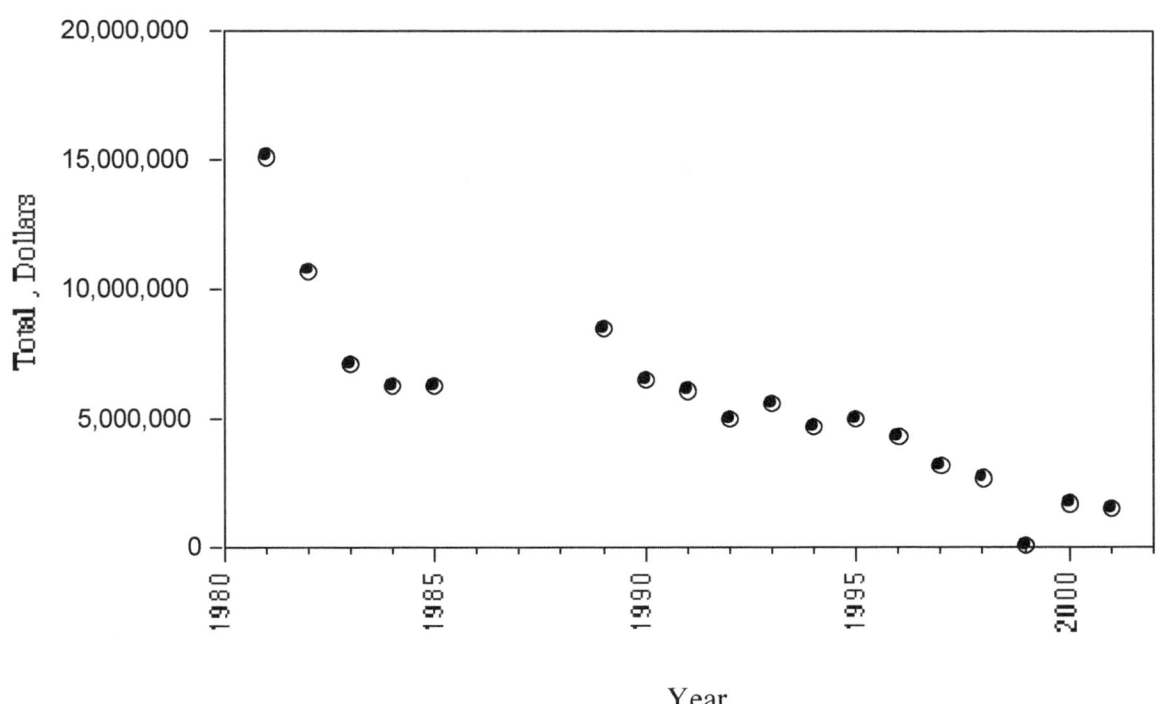

Figure 18. Landings of oysters, soft shell clams, and blue mussels in Great South Bay.

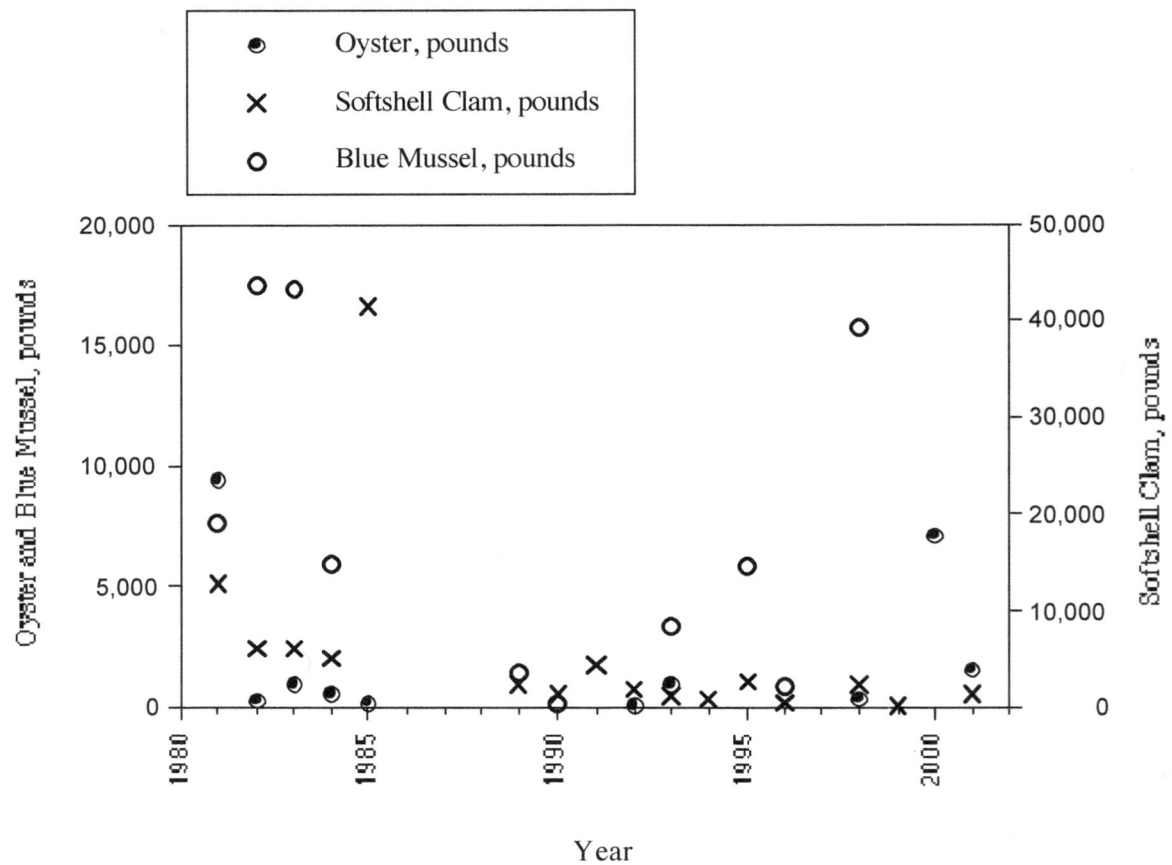

Figure 19. Landings of blue crabs in GSB. The data shown with circles are the NMFS landings data. The permit data is the blue crab catch as reported on the following year's commercial crabbing application.

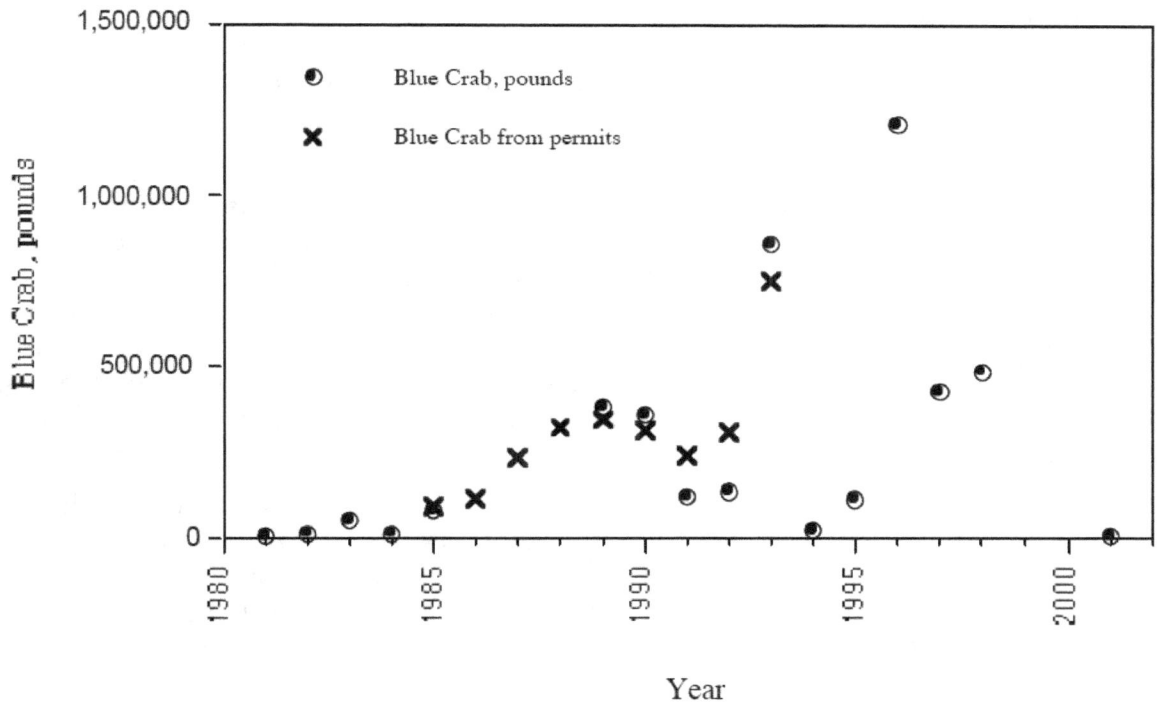

Figure 20. Landings of bluefish and weakfish in GSB.

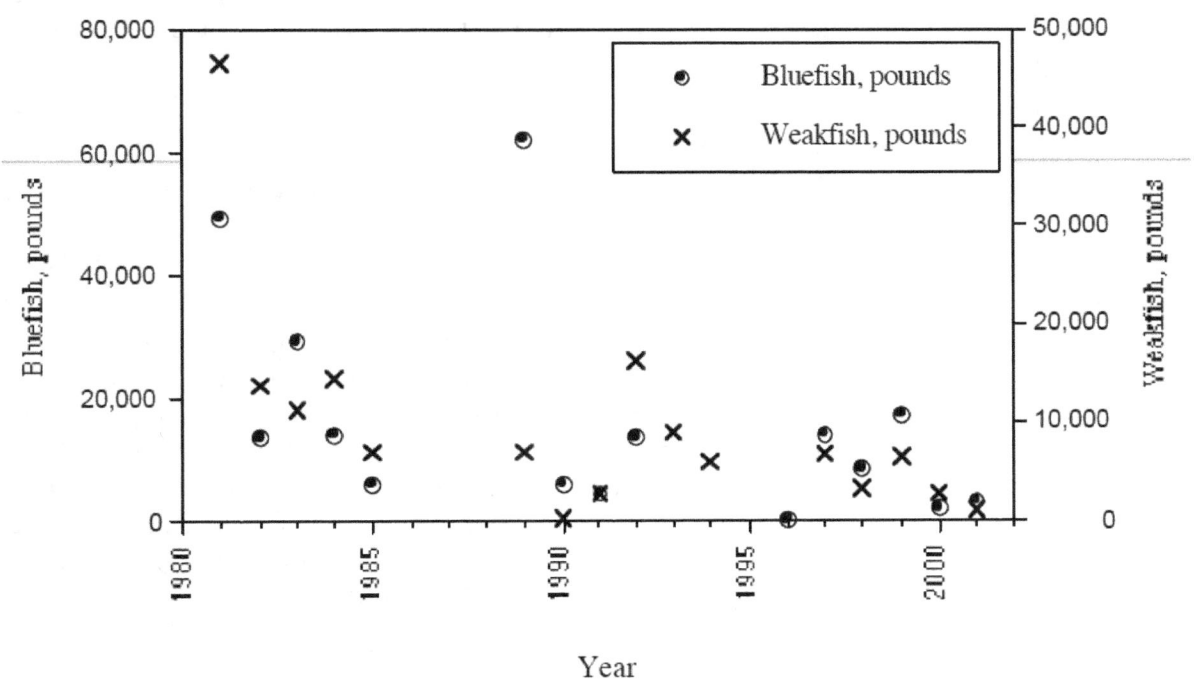

RESEARCH NEEDS

The GSB is in some ways very well studied, while there are also major uncertainties due to a lack of investigation. A number of studies in particular can be recommended that would significantly add to our understanding of GSB. The recommendations are given below in no particular order of priority. The effort that would be required to conduct these studies varies significantly and no particular consideration is given to the resources that would be needed to conduct them.

1. The data that has been collected since 1976 by Suffolk County is a very rich database including physical properties, nutrients, coliforms, and even brown tide counts. The length of the record, the number of stations taken, and the frequency of the measurements provide a great opportunity to learn more about GSB. It would be worthwhile to commit persons to a detailed analysis of this data. It would also be advisable to encourage and assist if necessary the county to continue the collection in order to assure that the time series (a relatively rare look at change in a coastal ecosystem over time) continues.

2. There appears to be no recent maps of eelgrass distribution and density. As it is clear that the distribution and density of seagrasses has varied significantly over time, old maps of distribution may no longer be accurate. Projects to map eelgrass distribution and density would be valuable. If these were repeated at, say, a five year interval, such studies would give a valuable look at eelgrass changes in response to environmental factors.

3. While there appears to be little concern from toxic contaminants, a broadened program to establish contamination levels, especially in the FIIS area itself, would seem prudent. The latest EPA monitoring under the National Coastal Assessment will add some information on contamination in GSB. Nevertheless, the data will still be scant, and at least the prior EPA monitoring did not include analysis of any agricultural chemicals.

4. The coliform bacteria levels in GSB are probably monitored well enough to assure that conditions at the major beaches are within regulatory standards. However, the monitoring is insufficient to determine the sources of contamination. Especially notable is a lack of sampling in relation to boating activities. Boating was implicated in an earlier brief study as the primary source of contamination on the north shore of Prie Island.

5. The populations of commercially and recreationally taken species, other than hard clams, are little known, and abundance trends must be derived from reported commercial harvests. These are is a very imprecise and perhaps completely misleading indicator for some species. It would be desirable to have a monitoring program that provided a direct and objective measure of the abundance of finfish and shellfish. For the one species whose abundance is monitored carefully, the hard clam, the towns' monitoring programs stop at the political boundaries so they do not cover the FIIS waters, nor the large area managed by the Blue Point Company.

6. The brief analysis of the trends in chlorophyll and dissolved inorganic nitrogen provided in this report indicate that the primary producing organisms, and probably the production itself, of the Bay have changed significantly since the last measurements of primary production in the GSB. New studies of primary production may provide some insight into the dynamics of the harvestable populations of the Bay, and it would help demonstrate the effects of the sewage management initiatives on Long Island on GSB.

ACKNOWLEDGEMENTS

A great deal of this report was dependent upon two data sets. I thank David Sutherland of the National Marine Fisheries Service for culling out and providing the landings data for Great South Bay. I thank Bob Nuzzi and Robert Waters of Suffolk County New York for providing a copy of the extensive data set generated by the county. This work was funded by the National Park Service, administered through the North Atlantic Coast Cooperative Ecosystem Studies Unit at the University of Rhode Island.

LITERATURE CITED

Bokuniewicz H, Schubel JR (1991) The origin and development of Great South Bay: A geological perspective. In: Schubel JR, Bell TM, Carter HH (eds) The Great South Bay. State University of New York Press, Stony Brook, New York, p 5-7

Bokuniewicz H, McElroy A, Schlenk C, Tanski J (1993) Estuarine Resources of the Fire Island National Seashore and Vicinity. New York Sea Grant, Stony Brook, New York

Bricelj VM (1996) Ecological impacts of brown tide. McElroy A Brown Tide Summit New York Sea Grant

Bricelj VM, Lonsdale DJ (1997) *Aureococcus anophagefferens*: Causes and ecological consequences of brown tides in U.S. mid-Atlantic coastal waters. Limnology and Oceanography 42:1023-1038

Buchman MF (1999) NOAA Screening Quick Reference Tables. 99-1, National Oceanic and Atmospheric Administration, Seattle

Carpenter EJ, Brinkhuis BM, Capone DG (1991) Primary production and nitrogenous nutrients in Great South Bay. In: Schubel JR, Bell TM, Carter HH (eds) The Great South Bay. State University of New York Press, Stony Brook, New york, p 33-42

Castro LR (1990) Early life history of bay anchovy in Great South Bay, NY: Factors affecting recruitment. Master of Science Thesis. Marine Environmental Sciences State University of New York at Stony Brook

Clark LB (2000) Temporal and Spatial Distributions of Trace Metals, Organic Carbon, and Inorganic Nutrients in a Barrier Island Estuary: The Great South Bay System. Master of Science Thesis. Marine Environmental Sciences State University of New York at Stony Brook

Conley DC (2000) Numerical Modeling of Fire island Storm Breach Impacts Upon Circulation and Water Quality of Great South Bay, NY. 124, Marine Sciences Research Center, State University of New York, Stony Brook

Cosper E, Dennison W, Carpenter E, Bricelj V, Mitchell J, Kuenstner S, Colflesh D, Dewey M (1987) Recurrent and persistent brown tide blooms perturb coastal marine ecosystem. Estuaries 10:284-290

Gobler C, Sanudo-Wilhelmy S (2001) Effects of organic carbon, organic nitrogen, inorganic nutrients, and iron additions on the growth of phytoplankton and bacteria during a brown tide bloom. Marine Ecology Progress Series 209:19-34

Gobler CJ, Renaghan MJ, Buck NJ (2002) Impacts of nutrients and grazing mortality on the abundance of Aureococcus anophagefferens during a New York brown tide bloom. Limnology and Oceanography 47:129-141

Green R (1972) Wetlands on Long Island. The Center for the Environment of Man, Hartford

Greene GT, Mirchel ACF, Behrens WJ, Becker DS (1977) surficial sediments and seagrass of eastern Great South Bay, NY. 12, State University of New York at Stony Brook, Stony Brook, New York

Greenfield D, Lonsdale D (2002) Mortality and growth of juvenile hard clams *Mercenaria mercenaria* during brown tide. Marine Biology 141:1045-1050

Hair ME, Buckner S (1973) An Assessment of the Water Quality characteristics of Great South Bay and Contiguous Streams. Adelphi University Institute of marine Science, Garden city, Long Island, New York

Hinga KR, Stanley DW, Klein CJ, Lucid DT, Katz MJ (eds) (1991) The National Estuarine Eutrophication Project: Workshop Proceedings. National Oceanic and Atmospheric Administration, Silver Spring, MD

Hinga KR, Jeon H, Lewis NF (1995) Marine eutrophication review-Part 1: Quantifying the effects of nitrogen enrichment on phytoplankton in coastal ecosystems. No. 4, NOAA Coastal Ocean Office, Silver Spring, MD

Kana TW (1995) A mesoscale sediment budget for Long Island, New York. Marine Geology 126:87-110

Kassner J, Cerrato R, Carrano T (1991) Toward understanding and improving the abundance of quahogs (*Mercenaria mercenaria*) in the eastern Great South Bay, New York. Rice MA, Grady M, Schwartz ML Proceedings of The First Rhode Island Shellfish Conference

Kassner J, Squires D (1991) The Baymen. In: Schubel JR, Bell TM, Carter HH (eds) The Great South Bay. State University of New York Press, Stony Brook, New York, p 65-74

Keller AA, Rice RL (1989) Effects of nutrient enrichment on natural populations of the brown tide phytopolankton *Aureococcus anophagefferens* (Chrysophyceae). Journal of Phycology 25:636-646

Koppelman L (1991) A Management Approach. In: Schubel JR, Bell TM, Carter HH (eds) The Great South Bay. State University of New York Press, Stony Brook, New York, p 89-100

Larson AA (2000) The Role of Substrate Type in Characterizing the Community Parameters and the Distribution of *Mercenaria mercenaria* (L.) in Great South Bay, New York. Master of Science Thesis. Marine Environmental Sciences State University of New York at Stony Brook

Leatherman SP (1985) Geommorphic and stratographic analysis of Fire Island. Marine Geology 63:173-195

Lively J, Kaufman, Carpenter EJ (1983) Phytoplankton ecology of a barrier island estuary: Great South Bay, New York. Estuarine Coastal and Shelf Science 16:51-68

Lomas M, Glibert P, Clougherty D, Huber DJ, J, Alexander J, Haramoto E (2001) Elevated organic nutrient ratios associated with brown tide algal blooms of *Aureococcus anophagefferens* (Pelagophyceae). Journal of Plankton Research 23:1339-1344

Maher NP, Cerrato R (2000) Baseline Sedimentary And Faunal Characteristics Of Potential Shell Planting And Reference Sites In Great South Bay. 126, Marine Sciences Research Center, State University Of New York at Stony Brook, Stony Brook, New York

McElroy A (ed) (1996) Proceedings of the Brown Tide Summit, October 20-21, 1995. New York Sea Grant,

McHugh JL (1991) The Hard Clam Fishery Past and Present. In: Schubel JR, Bell TM, Carter

HH (eds) The Great South Bay. State University of New York Press, Stony Brook, New York, p 55-64

McNulty CA (1989) Water quality Monitoring Program summer 1988 Fire Island National Seashore. U.S. Department of Interior, National Park Service, Fire Island National Seashore, Patchogue, NY

Merson R (1999) Nursery Grounds and Maturation of the Sandbar Shark in the Western North Atlantic. Dissertation Thesis. University of Rhode Island, 02882

Mulholland M, Gobler C, Lee C (2002) Peptide hydrolysis, amino acid oxidation, and nitrogen uptake in communities seasonally dominated by *Aureococcus anophagefferens*. Limnology and Oceanography 47:1094-1108

Nixon SW, Granger SL, Taylor DI, Johnson PW, Buckley BA (1994) Subtidal volume fluxes, nutrient inputs and the brown tide--An alternate hypothesis. Estuar Coast Shelf Sci 39:303-312

Nixon S (1995) Coastal Marine Eutrophication: A definition, social causes, and future concerns. Ophelia 41:199-219

Papa S (1994) Distribution and Abundance of the Hard Clam in Relation to Environmental Characteristics in Eastern Great South Bay, New York. Master of Science Thesis. Marine Environmental Sciences University of New York at Stony Brook

Pilson MEQ (1985) On the residence time of water in Narragansett Bay. Estuaries 8:2-14

Raposa KB, Oviatt CA (2000) The Influence of Contiguous Shoreline Type, Distance from Shore, and Vegetation Biomass on Nekton Community Structure in Eelgrass Beds. Estuaries 23:46-55

Saville T (1962) Report on factors affecting the population of Great South Bay, Long Island, NY with special reference to algal blooms. Report to Jones Beach Parkway Authority, Babylon, NY.

Schubel JR, Bell TM, Carter HH (eds) (1991) The Great South Bay. State University of New York Press, Stony Brook, New york

Short F, Muehlstein L, Porter D (1987) Eelgrass Wasting disease: Causes and recurrence of a marine epidemic. Biological Bulletin 173:557-562

Steinback JMK (1999) The Ocean Beach Invertebrates of Fire Island National Seashore, New York: Spatial and Temporal Trends and the Effects of Vehicular Disturbance. Master of Sciences Thesis. Marine Environmental Sciences State University of New York at Stony Brook

Tanski J, Bokuniewicz H, Schlenk C (eds) (2001) Impacts of barrier island breaches on selected biological resources of Great South Bay, New York: final report. New York Sea Grant, Stony Brook, NY

Wallace HVE (1991) A Comparison of Hard Clam Population Characteristics Between High and Low Density Regions Within Great South Bay. Thesis. Marine Environmental Sciences State University of New York at Stony Brook

Ward T (1993) Bathymetric Influences On Current Patterns In Shallow Coastal

Environments. Master of Science Thesis. Marine Environmental Sciences State University of New York at Stony Brook

Wilson RE, Wong KC, Carter HH (1991) Aspects of Circulation and Exchange in Great South Bay. In: Schubel JR, Bell TM, Carter HH (eds) The Great South Bay. State University of New York Press, Stony Brook, New york, p 9-22.

As the nation's primary conservation agency, the Department of the Interior has responsibility for most of our nationally owned public land and natural resources. This includes fostering sound use of our land and water resources; protecting our fish, wildlife, and biological diversity; preserving the environmental and cultural values of our national parks and historical places; and providing for the enjoyment of life through outdoor recreation. The department assesses our energy and mineral resources and works to ensure that their development is in the best interests of all our people by encouraging stewardship and citizen participation in their care. The department also has a major responsibility for American Indian reservation communities and for people who live in island territories under U.S. administration.

NPS D-111 September 2005